This Changes
Nothing

TORN CURTAIN PUBLISHING
Auckland, New Zealand
www.torncurtainpublishing.com

ISBN Softcover 978-1-991299-91-8
ISBN EPub 978-1-991299-92-5

This book is not intended as a substitute for professional counseling or medical advice.

Unless noted, all scripture quotations in this publication are from the New King James Version. Copyright © 1982 by Thomas Nelson, Inc. Used by permission. All rights reserved.

Scripture quotations marked ESV are taken from The Holy Bible, English Standard Version®, copyright © 2001 by Crossway, a publishing ministry of Good News Publishers. Used by permission. All rights reserved.

Scripture quotations marked AMP are taken from the Amplified® Bible (AMP), Copyright © 1954, 1958, 1962, 1964, 1965, 1987 by The Lockman Foundation. Used by permission. www.lockman.org.

Scripture quotations marked NIV are taken from the New International Version®, NIV®. Copyright © 1973, 1978, 1984, 2011 by Biblica, Inc.™ Used by permission of Zondervan. All rights reserved worldwide.

Typeset in Garamond Pro, Didot, Agatha Pricilla and Raleway.
Cover image by Jeremy Lapak (Unsplash.com). Used with permission.

Cataloging in Publishing Data
   Title: This Changes Nothing: Recovering Your Faith When Life Has Thrown
      You Its Worst
   Author: Jessica Long
   Subjects: Christian living, Faith, Grief and loss, Emotional healing, Spiritual growth, Bible study, Coping with grief, Adversity and hardship, Mourning and comfort, Spiritual endurance, Family loss, Childhood loss and grief, Word of faith, Spiritual warfare, Pastoral resources, Christian counselling, Group study resources.

A copy of this title is held at the National Library of New Zealand.

This Changes Nothing.

RECOVERING YOUR FAITH
WHEN LIFE HAS THROWN
YOU ITS WORST.

JESSICA LONG

Foreword by Dr. B Best

Foreword

First, let me introduce you to our friends, the Long family. Pete, the father, is a leading architect in our city, plays bass guitar in the worship band at our church, and serves on our deacon board. His wife, Jessica, the author of this book, majored in child growth and development and has a rich history of working with children with developmental issues. She is a lead singer on our praise and worship team and is a speaker for women's conferences. Currently, their son Reese is a college student majoring in sports management. Their daughter, Charis, is a senior in a private Christian high school at the School of the Ozarks, where she is a member of the golf team. Each church service will always find her front row center, along with anywhere from four to ten of her teenage friends.

Of all the complex issues that walk through the door of a counselor or a pastor, very few, if any, match the complexity of the issues associated with helping a family deal with the death of a child. Psychologically, we as individuals expect to take care of our aging parents, eventually witnessing their death, and often, making arrangements for their memorial services. This is the normal sequence of life. Experiencing the death of a child is not the normal thing for a parent.

Seldom does one find a book about grief that describes the grieving process so that a layperson can understand, yet at the same time can be used to train professional workers in the grieving process. This book satisfies the needs of both groups. First, for the trained professional workers. The professionally trained worker will immediately recognize the five stages of grief as articulated by Kubler-Ross (Denial, Anger, Bargaining, Depression, and Acceptance) as Jessica experiences them and passes through them, often more than once. For the untrained, this book exposes the raw emotions that a parent experiences when they lose a child. They often feel like they are going to lose their minds, only to later discover their feelings were the norm for the experience. As an additional insight, the reader can learn helpful ways to support grieving parents by reading how others helped Jessica and her family in their time of need.

Finally, this book offers hope! The brutally honest and transparent way in which the book was written helps the reader understand the grieving process and to realize there is hope for healing in the future.

— **Dr. Berl H. Best**
Licensed Professional Counselor

Contents

Prologue

"I need to call my husband."

"Don't leave just yet," the nurse replied. "The oncologist wants to see you."

Tears streaming down my face, I walked across the hallway and entered the room where the doctor was waiting. He pulled up a seat.

"I need to go over a few things with you, Jessica. They're not pleasant."

I tried to stay grounded. Logically, I needed to make some decisions. "Would you like the hospital to conduct an autopsy?" I listened to the details. "It's not essential, but we recommend it. It might help you later on if we can confirm the cause of death." The oncologist was quick to assure me his body was not going to be disfigured in any way. "It's not cutting his body up, it's just like taking biopsies of each organ."

I didn't care. I realize this may sound cold, but I'd seen my son's dead body just a few minutes earlier.

He was gone. It didn't matter what they did now.

I asked if I could call my husband.

"Of course."

The doctor handed me the phone and walked outside for a minute.

That's when it struck me. Pete was back at home in Missouri by himself.

I didn't want him to hear the news when he was alone.

My first call was to my pastors, Guy and Barb. Guy had married Pete and I nine years earlier. He and Barb were our best friends. We'd spent countless hours together over the years. I was the worship leader and Pete was the youth pastor at their church. They'd celebrated Keagan's birth with us four years earlier, and our second son, Reece's, birth three years after that.

Guy answered the phone.

"He didn't make it," I said. "He's gone."

It was the worst news to ever come out of my mouth, and I didn't know how else to say it.

It almost felt shameful.

Guy had been standing in faith with us for Keagan's healing from the minute we'd heard the doctor utter the word 'leukemia'.

"Wait," I'd said two weeks earlier when the diagnosis was first spoken. "We need to pray right now! We are speaking about *leukemia,* and I want us to speak *life.*"

Guy had placed his hand on my shoulder, as if to slow things down.

"Is that okay with you?" he asked the doctor.

He'd prayed with us right there and then. We were determined to believe that our four-year-old son would be supernaturally healed.

Two weeks to the day, Keagan was gone.

I heard the thump of the phone as it hit the ground, followed by muffled crying.

It touched me deeply to hear my pastors grieving my child's death as if it were their own. In that moment, I felt so loved—and, strangely, comforted.

I never realized that shared grief could feel so reassuring. *We were not alone. Someone else would be walking through this with us.*

Pastor Guy picked up the phone, still crying.

"I'm so sorry, Jessica," he said.

I waited ten or fifteen minutes, then called Pete.

"Is Guy there?" I asked when he picked up the phone.

"Yeah," Pete said, "He just pulled in." As Guy walked in the door, I broke the news.

"Pete, I'm so sorry," I said through tears. "He didn't make it."

I couldn't see Pete's response on the other end of the phone. All I know is that when Guy walked through the door and saw Pete's expression, he collapsed to the floor once again in grief. In that moment, Pete felt as overwhelmed by our pastor's love as I had.

"I'm so, so sorry," I apologized again.

Keagan was gone? Pete tried to wrap his head around what I was saying, but none of it made sense.

Finally, a coherent thought entered his mind. *This isn't right.*

There were no words. Just two of us, one on either end of the phone, sobbing our hearts out, and our pastor down on the floor, grieving with us.

I

Death Is Not an Option

From the moment I heard the diagnosis, I decided death wasn't an option. *God was our healer.*

This wasn't just something I believed—it was an active statement of faith. *My son was not going to die.* I was standing in agreement with God's Word, believing it in my heart, and most of all, speaking it out.

Our response to any challenge we faced had always been, "God is able. We're believing for breakthrough." Then we thanked Him in advance for what He would do.

When we were struggling financially, that was our response. My husband, Pete, and I opened the scriptures, took God's promises at face value, and confidently declared His provision over our lives. Instead of fretting or speaking doubt-filled words like, "We never have enough money to pay the bills," Pete and I spoke in faith: "God, you provide for our needs according to your riches. Thank you that we have enough to pay our bills *and* give to every good work!"

We believed that the most important thing about faith was that our words aligned with what we knew to be true, despite how difficult a situation may have looked. Our words changed our thinking, shifted our attitudes, and they were certainly powerful because, eventually, God always came through.

So, of course, when our family was suddenly faced with a terrible diagnosis, our response was the same. *God was the author of life. He would come through for our son.* Of that, we had no doubt.

Our natural response was faith.

Our First Response

I didn't need convincing that faith and action worked together. I knew that faith requires both believing *and* doing. There is a spiritual component *and* a natural, physical component.

When we were unemployed, we didn't just pray for a job, then sit at home waiting for a job to come. We looked for work. We applied for jobs. We showed up at interviews.

But our *first* response was faith.

When we were sick, we didn't just pray for healing and ignore the symptoms. We went to the doctor. We took the tests.

But our *first* response was faith.

And so, when we received the results of the blood tests and heard that our son had leukemia, faith was our natural, immediate response. Even as the doctor began explaining the diagnosis, I stopped him. "We need to pray," I insisted. "There is no way we are going to submit to this. God is going to come through for us. Our son is going to live." I was speaking in faith what my heart already believed: *Death is not an option.*

The scenario we were facing marked a pinnacle of faith for us as a family. "We are believing for the life *of our child!*" I whispered in Pete's ear one night as we lay on a narrow little air mattress on the floor of the hospital room. "When Keagan is healed, there will be nothing we can't believe God for. Finances, relationships, health, our future . . . we will never struggle again! The devil will rue the day he messed with our family."

Faith and Compassion

As humans, when we hear the worst, we naturally want to grasp for something. For Pete and me, it was prayer—and the power of faith to move mountains. I took what God said in the Bible about healing and spoke it out in agreement. I stood in faith to the best of my ability. There was nothing else I could have done. Keagan didn't make it, but I'll never regret giving it my best shot.

We'd already decided death was not on the map, but the fear was still there. Leukemia is a big diagnosis. It's not the same thing as a cold or the flu. It's like standing in front of a mountain and knowing it's going to take every bit of physical energy you have to climb it and get to the summit. We could feel the weight of the diagnosis, but harder still was seeing our son's reaction to the nurses. Whenever they came to check on him, he would yell at them to get away from him. We were dealing with feelings none of us had ever faced before.

Hospitals can be a scary place for a four-year-old. We didn't want to frighten Keagan with words like *chemotherapy* or *leukemia* that he wouldn't understand. We explained that the blood inside his veins was making him feel sick, and that was why he had to be in the hospital for a while. But we wanted him to focus on getting better and not worrying, so we told him very little else. I don't believe Keagan ever heard us say the word leukemia—not once. I didn't want the word in his vocabulary. Instead, we told him stories of faith.

One of Keagan's favorite bible stories was *David and Goliath*. He'd always loved acting it out, but he'd never agree to act the part of Goliath. "No, you be Goliath, I want to be David!" he insisted. Now, as we sat on the edge of our son's hospital bed, holding his hand, the analogy captured Keagan's imagination. "Right now, you get to be David!" we told him. Keagan understood. He needed to trust God that he would get better, like David trusted God when he fought Goliath.

"I wish I had a slingshot to throw rocks at the sickness!" Keagan said.

"Your *words* are like rocks," I encouraged him. "Throw 'em!"

I gave my son words to say.

"I'm healed!"

"God is healing me!"

"Jesus took stripes on His back so I could be healed."

He giggled as he repeated the phrases after me.

And then something arose within us. Soon, we weren't just fighting for Keagan. We wanted the entire ward to be healed! Pete and I decided the devil was going to want us out of that hospital as soon as possible because we were going to bring such light to that place. We weren't going to settle for sickness or disease or death. We were going to pray for everyone! We wanted healing for every child in that hospital, including ours. Every time we heard an announcement that a child was being discharged, we turned to each other and said, "Thank you, God, for allowing that child to go home. Thank you for healing that child!" And then we declared with Keagan, "We're next!" Our faith was unshakeable.

It wasn't just our family's faith that was activated—others were standing in faith too.

And when faith rises, so does compassion.

When friends from our church in Branson, Missouri, heard the news, they picked up our car and drove it to Memphis, Tennessee, where Keagan was being treated, so that we would have transportation while we were there. Our pastor's wife and her eight-year-old daughter visited us, bringing cards and a few gifts from people back home. Then they asked if they could take our one-year-old son, Reece, so that we could focus on Keagan. *Just like family,* we thought. We waved goodbye to our youngest son, then began reading all the notes and messages from our church family.

It's an amazing thing to feel the love of others during the worst times of your life. Our friends stood with us in faith, but it was their acts of compassion and generosity that propped us up. To see their love displayed so tangibly in acts of kindness and compassion was a beautiful light in the middle of such terrible darkness.

We wanted to convey the same love and compassion to the other families in the hospital. We were believing for every child on the ward to be healed, but as we looked into the faces of their parents and carers, we felt what they felt. Our kid was in there, but theirs was too. I remember a single mom who had no way to leave the hospital and get to the store. We offered to pray for her and her child. "If there's anything you need," we said, "just let us know. You don't need to pay us a thing. Our friend can stay with Keagan awhile. Do you need a toothbrush? Do you need laundry detergent? Is there anything we can get for you? How about your favorite drink or snack?" We were determined to be light and love to those around us and dispel all darkness in that place.

As compassion filled us, our faith continued to rise. Pete and I didn't just want Keagan to be healed—we were determined to give the devil a black eye. We'd make sure he was sorry he ever messed with our son! As we walked down the hospital hallways, we stopped at each room and offered to pray for each child. We felt sure that God would help us, and that by the time we were able to return home, there would be a multitude of kiddos released and disease-free!

II

Desperate Prayers

Two Weeks Earlier . . .

The only indication that Keagan might be unwell was that he came home from daycare with a great big bruise on his back. We didn't notice it until we were giving him a bath that night. Right away, I called the daycare center. "What on earth happened?" I asked. "Did he hurt himself today? He's got a massive big bruise!" The director assured me nothing serious had happened. Keagan had stood up in a play structure and hit his back on the edge of it, but he didn't seem to be in pain. It was nothing they would have written an accident report for or notified the parents about. He just said, "Ow", rubbed his back, and went on playing.

A few days later, Keagan started running a fever, so we decided to have him checked out just to be on the safe side. As the examination progressed, so did the sense of worry and fear. When the doctor began feeling Keagan's abdomen and mentioned that his spleen seemed enlarged, I began asking questions. *Why would it be enlarged? What could be causing that?* I glimpsed the concern on the doctor's face. "It can only be one of two things," he replied. "Let's run some tests and see what's going on." But I didn't want to wait; I wanted to know what the doctor was thinking. "Tell me the truth. I need to know what I'm dealing with," I replied. When he answered, "It's either mono or leukemia," my mind immediately went to mono (*mononucleosis, or glandular fever*). There was no way my son could have leukemia!

Within a few hours, the blood results confirmed the worst. "I've spoken with a pediatric oncologist at St. Jude's," the doctor said. "They're waiting to admit Keagan this afternoon." *St Jude's? That wasn't a local hospital. St. Jude's was in Memphis, Tennessee!* We raced home and threw a few personal things into suitcases, trying to think of everything we would need in between crying and trying to wrap our heads around what had just happened. By the time Pete and I arrived at the airport with our two young sons, a family from our church was already there to meet us. Wrapping their arms around us, they shoved money into our hands and prayed with us. Minutes later, we boarded a medical flight to St. Jude's.

Keagan was taken directly to intensive care, where a team of doctors and nurses began inserting needles into his little body. One tried to draw blood, another was inserting a PICC line under Keagan's clavicle so he could receive chemotherapy, while another was hooking him up to monitors and machines. Pete held onto Reece while I stood at the entrance of the room, aghast. There was nothing I could do. I felt so guilty, so ashamed that I couldn't help my child in the moment he needed me the most. It tore me apart inside. Keagan was screaming. He wanted me to save him. I could read it in his eyes. I could see the desperation on his face, begging me as if to say, *Why aren't you helping? Why aren't you doing something?* He was looking at me like I had thrown him to the wolves.

I tried to reassure him, but Keagan couldn't hear me. He was screaming and thrashing around on the bed, trying to get to me. Suddenly, I couldn't handle any more. I couldn't hold back the tears, but I knew that if Keagan saw me crying, it would make it worse. My husband looked at me and read me like a book. "I've got this," he said with his eyes. "I can handle it."

With my son's screams and cries ringing in my ears, I slipped out into the hallway and broke into heaving sobs. I felt so small and powerless. I'd always made things better in the past. Now, there was nothing I could do. I knew what was happening in there had to be done, *but my son was only four years old!* We hadn't even had a chance to tell him he was sick. I felt like the most horrible mom in the world, walking out of the room while all he wanted was for me to rescue him from these horrible people who were poking and prodding him.

◆ ◆ ◆

The following two weeks were a blur. Keagan stayed in the intensive care unit for a week before he was transferred to a regular room. "It's looking okay," one of the doctors explained. "The type of leukemia Keagan has is one of the most curable kinds. There's an 80% chance of full recovery." We took that news happily. I remember praying, "They have given him an 80% chance of recovery, but with you, God, it's 180%!" As Pete and I settled into the hospital room with Keagan and our little toddler, Reece, our faith rose. "We believe that you are working in Keagan's body right now to bring healing. We trust you and know you paid for his healing on the cross. We declare him healed and whole in Jesus' name."

Sure enough, the following day, Keagan's white cell count began coming down, his spleen seemed to be recovering, and Keagan was back to his talkative self. The day care center where Keagan attended sent a little box of cards and well-wishes. Keagan couldn't read, but he could recognize his friends' names on the drawings, and as we pinned them up on the wall by his bed, Pete and I were full of faith. Our child was going to be healed, along with every child on that ward! We were determined!

Finally, Keagan was discharged to the Ronald McDonald House just a block away from the hospital. "You'll need to come back and forth for chemo treatments for a few months, but after that, you should be able to return home and travel back for checkups."

At that point, we decided it was best for Pete to head back home. He would work for a few weeks, then we'd swap, and I would go back to work for a few weeks. Our bosses were understanding, and we figured we could just trade off and on like that until Keagan had finished his course of treatment.

◆ ◆ ◆

After we said our goodbyes, I took Keagan into the kitchen to make him something to eat. Having just finished his first round of chemotherapy, he wasn't super hungry. I sat him up on the counter while I started preparing a quick meal, but for a moment, I stood eye-to-eye in front of him. I lost focus on the food as his gentle blue eyes met mine. His small hands reached out to cup my face tenderly, and patting my cheek gently, he said, "You are a good mom." My melting heart pocketed those words. I felt so proud that Keagan could express his feelings. With a degree in child development and years of experience working with preschoolers, I knew that four-year-olds are often egocentric and reluctant to give compliments. Wrapping him in a tight hug, I told him, "I love you too, and you are a good son!"

That night, Keagan snuggled up to me as he fell asleep. Eventually, I moved to the bed beside his and went to sleep. But in the early morning hours, I woke to hear Keagan moaning, "My stomach is hurting." Getting up, I went over and kissed my lips to his forehead. It didn't seem like he had a temperature. I picked up the card we had been given earlier that day, outlining the side effects of chemotherapy. *Stomach pain, queasiness, vomiting.* That must be what was happening. The card advised placing warm towels against the child's body. *Towels. Where could I get warm towels?* There were a few towels in the bathroom, but no dryer to make them warm.

Suddenly, I felt frantic. Why hadn't anyone given me a tour of the building? I had no idea what floor the laundry room was on. "Wait here," I said to Keagan. I felt like screaming as I ran into the hallway, "Somebody help me!" But everyone was asleep, and I didn't know who to contact.

I ran downstairs to the front desk, but no one was there. I ran back up again, searching the rooms on our floor. It seemed to take forever. Finally, I stumbled across the laundry room, threw our towels into the dryer, and ran back to the room to check on Keagan.

Keagan was clutching his stomach and crying in pain. I wished someone were there to help me, but there was no one. "I'll be right back," I said, running out into the hallway again, tears streaming down my face. Less than a minute later, I was back in the room, holding the warm towels on Keagan's stomach. "Do you need to go to the bathroom?" I asked. "I don't know . . . maybe?" he replied. Carefully, we walked to the bathroom. He had a huge bowel movement. *Whew,* I thought. *That's all it was.* Climbing back into bed, we tried to go to sleep again. But within a matter of minutes, Keagan started throwing up all over the bed. *Another side effect.* Sitting Keagan in a soft chair, I pulled the comforter off the bed and began searching for fresh blankets and sheets.

Keagan said he felt better now, but I could tell that he was not well at all. He was pale and shivering, and this time when I felt his head, he was running a fever. I called the hospital. "Bring him in right away," the nurse said. "Fever is a sign of infection, and he needs white blood cells to fight it. The chemotherapy targets the white blood cells and wipes them out. If it's an infection, it could be very dangerous."

Keagan was not a small four-year-old. I was out of breath, and Keagan was groaning and moaning as I struggled to carry him down the flight of stairs and through the parking lot. Finally, I got him into his car seat and made our way onto the street. The hospital was only a short drive away, but I could see Keagan was beginning to lose consciousness. I began talking louder and louder, asking him questions to keep him awake.

I don't know why I didn't drive straight to the emergency entrance. Instead, I pulled into the hospital parking lot, thinking, *How will I ever carry him all the way from the parking lot to the front doors of the hospital?* Thankfully, right in front of my parking space was a little red wagon, designed especially for the children to ride in. Usually, they were kept just inside the foyer of St. Jude's hospital. "Thank you, God!"

I sensed an urgency in my spirit as I placed Keagan in the wagon. "Hang on, Keagan! Mom is going to run," I told him. He held on in a daze as I ran towards the hospital entrance.

The nurses were ready for us. Quickly, they hooked Keagan up to the monitors and started him on antibiotics. By now, he was having trouble breathing. "It's going to be okay," I reassured him. "These people are going to take care of things."

"Stop saying that!" he snapped back at me.

I was shocked. Keagan had always been a compliant child. He wasn't a fighter. He wasn't easily annoyed. I remembered one of the nurses telling me, "Steroids can make kids a little mean, so be prepared." Maybe it was that . . . or maybe he knew something we didn't. Thankfully, he soon calmed down. Sitting beside him, I held his hand and he closed his eyes as the nurses kept working on him. "I'm glad he's resting," I whispered. Keagan seemed to be drifting off when he gave a sudden little gasp, as if he'd just seen something in a dream.

"Magic Kingdom," he breathed sleepily. I looked at him, surprised to hear him say anything, let alone something pleasant. It seemed so out of place after such an ordeal. The nurse turned and smiled. "Aww . . . that's a nice dream," she said.

I didn't know it then, but those would be his last words.

Within minutes, his foot began to twitch. A nurse pushed a button, and suddenly, nurses and doctors began flooding into the room. Seeing me there, one of the doctors turned to a nurse and asked, "Could you take Mom and get her a Sprite?"

"No! I'm not leaving," I told him. "I'm not thirsty, I'm staying right here."

The doctor began moving me to the door. "The waiting room is right across the hallway. We need you to stay there and trust us to do our job." A nurse came into the waiting room with me, and a few minutes later, a Catholic priest and a social worker joined her.

I sat down in a chair and cried hard. Someone handed me a phone. My hands were shaking as I dialed Pete. "Something is going on," I said through gritted teeth. "I don't know what's happening, but it's bad and I need you to pray for your son like you've never prayed before." Then I called my pastors and told them the same thing. I was brief and very adamant. When I hung up the phone, I stood to my feet. It was time to go to war.

III

Toe-to-Toe With the Devil

The priest, the nurse, and the social worker were quiet as I hung up the phone. The sense was that they were there to support me, to pick me up in case I crumbled. What they weren't prepared for was a mom who was going to war for the life of her child. "I don't know what you all believe or are used to," I told them tentatively, "but I'm getting ready to pray in tongues, and it will be loud." I didn't want to offend them or cause them to feel uncomfortable. "Please step out if you need to, it won't offend me at all."

The Catholic priest was the first to respond. "No, I'm going to stay right here," he said. "You do what you need to do." The nurse and the social worker nodded in agreement. I started out, "God, your wisdom is way beyond mine. I don't know what's happening in there. I can't touch it with my head, but I know that you know, so I'm going to pray in tongues and just ask you to guide my prayer." Then I took off, praying from my spirit. It was unintelligible to anyone else in the room, but my spirit was communicating with God's Spirit in that moment.

I prayed in tongues until a distinct word or picture came into my mind. Then I'd switch back into English. "Jesus, you paid for Keagan's healing on the cross." I began declaring. "God, your Word says that Christ has redeemed us from *every* curse—every sin, every sickness, poverty, even death! On the cross, Jesus took the curse for us, for it is written, *Cursed is every man that hangs on a tree.* I stand on your Word. Every blessing is ours in Christ!" I kept quoting scriptures and claiming physical life for my son for all I was worth.

I prayed in tongues again, and suddenly, I found my mind turning to the doctors. "God, you said, if any man lacks wisdom, let him ask of God who will give it liberally. I ask you to give the doctors supernatural wisdom as they work on my son. Guide their thoughts and their hands as they figure out what is happening. I thank you for their dedication, but God, your Word is above their word. They've given their diagnosis, but I choose to believe that you are the giver of life. You are the healer!" I wasn't about to give ground. I was contending for my son's healing.

I was praying loudly in tongues when the oncologist came into the waiting room. I paused as he spoke to me. "Jessica, I've been in there with Keagan. I just want to let you know that he's been having a hard time breathing, so we've had to intubate him. I'll come back and forth to keep you updated on what's happening."

As he turned to leave, I felt like I was being split in two. As a mom, my heart was broken. Physically, there was nothing I could do to help, and all I wanted to do was just sit and cry for what my son was enduring in the other room. I fell apart and sobbed as I pictured Keagan not being able to breathe and me not being there for him as the tubes were being inserted down his throat. But after thirty seconds or so, the spiritual side of me kicked back in. *Don't give up. Your faith is the answer! Pray for him and don't stop until they come and tell you that they have stabilized him.* Inwardly, I felt vicious and bear-like. I stood up out of that chair and began speaking directly to the devil. "Devil, you can't have my son!" I shouted. "Jesus shed His blood so that Keagan could be healed. You take your hands off him and leave now in Jesus' name. My son will live and not die. He will live to proclaim the goodness of God. He will live and testify to all that God is the healer!"

I felt like I was standing toe to toe with the devil. I was looking him straight in the face, and with the fierceness of a lion, I was roaring at him.

Every time the doctor popped back in, his updates would fuel my prayer. By now, I was alternating between praying in tongues, praying in English, and yelling at the devil. But when the oncologist came and told me Keagan's heart had stopped and the doctors were performing CPR, the mom part of me fell apart again, thinking about that flat line on the monitor and all those doctors pounding on his chest. "He's only four years old," I sobbed.

Then, thirty seconds later, I pulled myself back into fight mode. I shot back up out of the chair and onto my feet. I had no idea how to pray, so it was all in tongues. Then I had a moment of realization. I didn't need to beg or plead for healing. There was no need for desperation. I'd already prayed for my son's life. I'd bound the devil. There was nothing more to be said. It was as if I'd prayed it all out. When I tried to pray, nothing came to me. I'd given it everything I could. There was nothing left but to thank God that He had heard me and answered my cry.

◆ ◆ ◆

Throughout my life, I had been accused of being too loud, but I didn't care. I am a worshiper by nature. I was used to leading worship in church, so I was not ashamed or embarrassed to sing there in the hospital. It was as natural as prayer. Lifting my voice, I began singing:

I sing praises to your name, oh Lord,
Praises to your name, oh Lord,
For your name is great and greatly to be praised!

I was walking the floor, hands raised, belting out the praises of God, when the oncologist came back into the room. This time, instead of speaking, he fell into step and began to sing with me. It was like a breath of fresh air. I'd been contending alone in the hospital, and now there was someone beside me. I felt my faith join his as we walked, sang, and praised God together.

The nurse who had stayed with me fell to her knees. Her hands were lifted and trembling, and tears were running down her face. She, too, began singing with us. I noticed the Catholic priest and the social worker bow their heads and fold their hands in front of them as the presence of God filled the room. For a minute, I almost went over to pray for each of them, but I shook myself quickly and said, "No! I'm here to pray for my son! I'm not here to minister to them!"

Something powerful was taking place. I knew what I wanted to do, but I wasn't sure what God was doing. I often wish I could go back into that room and ask those people what they were feeling in that moment. I knew things weren't looking good. There had been no good report from the room across the hallway since my son had arrived at the hospital. When the oncologist left once more to check what was going on, I knew that the next time he returned, it could be to tell me that my son had died.

Preparing myself mentally, I decided that if that happened, I needed to be ready to raise my son from the dead. I began recalling accounts in scripture where someone was raised from the dead. *What did they do? Was there a formula? What words did they use?* I thought about how the prophet Elijah stretched himself out on top of a child's dead body three times, and the child came back to life. I recalled how Jesus took Jairus' daughter's hand and said, "Little girl, get up," and when Jesus spoke those words, her breath returned! I decided that if the doctors informed me that Keagan was dead, I wanted to be taken to him immediately, no time wasted. Until then, I would keep singing praises and praying.

Eventually, the oncologist did return, and his words were just as I had imagined. "Jessica, I'm so sorry. We tried for so long, and nothing worked. He's gone." I looked the doctor straight in the eye. "Take me to him right now," I replied. This was the moment I had prepared for. I was determined to raise my son from the dead.

But as I moved toward the door, the oncologist motioned to me. "Jessica, could you give them just five minutes? They need to clean him up." His words took me by surprise. *Clean him up? From what?* No, I wasn't having it. I didn't have time to mess with this man. I was on a mission. I tried to push past, but the oncologist stopped me. "Jessica, I need you to understand something. Keagan's blood was so thin that it's seeped out of his ears, nose, and mouth. We don't want you to see him that way. Give us five minutes to clean him up."

"Five minutes," I said, ". . . and not a second more."

A few minutes later, when I stepped out into the hallway, it was full of nurses. They had heard it all—the singing, the prayers, the praying in tongues. Now they were wiping tears from their faces. I had no idea why they were all looking at me, but I didn't have time to figure that out—I needed to get to my son! Soon, the door to Keagan's room opened, and one after another, Keagan's medical team began pouring out into the hallway, devastation on their faces. Their blue scrubs were soaked with sweat. Their hair hung wet and limp. Every one of them was crying.

Suddenly, I was overwhelmed with thankfulness for them. I could see how hard they had worked to save my son. Reaching out to touch their shoulder or shake their hands, I thanked them for how hard they had tried. I could tell how much they wished he had lived, too.

◆ ◆ ◆

I walked into the room. My son's body was lying on a table. Towels had been rolled up and placed all around his head and across his neck to soak up any blood that might seep out. The towels were fresh and white; I could tell they had just been placed there. Keagan's hair was dull; there was no color in his face. His eyes were open just a slit, but they were no longer a blue color. They were black. I was about to take his hand when I noticed his fingertips were already starting to turn brown. I'd meant to tell him to live in Jesus' name, but all that came out was, "You were supposed to live; you were supposed to live."

That's when I realized my son was not coming back. His body was there, but it felt as if his spirit had long gone. Perhaps he was already glimpsing heaven when he breathed the words, "Magic Kingdom."

Two nurses sat off to the side, crying. "It might not be easy," one of them said, "but if you want to hold him, we can help you do that." I told them that it was okay, my son wasn't there, it was just his body. I began crying, almost in disbelief. There were no words to say, nothing I could do. It felt awkward to be there with his body. It wasn't as if I was watching him as he slept. I stayed for about ten minutes, and then I left the room.

IV

God Is Still God

The hallway was calm when I stepped back out, but inside of me felt chaotic. *What had just happened?*

A part of me knew that something supernatural had taken place as we worshiped. The people in the waiting room down the hall felt it, the nurses at the nurses' station felt it. The doctors felt it. God had shown up.

But my son didn't get healed. It felt strange that that wasn't part of the package. It felt like it should have been.

A nurse came over to me. "Please don't leave just yet. The doctors need to talk to you." I agreed, but first, I had to call my husband, my pastors, and all the people who had been praying for us.

◆ ◆ ◆

I was holding it all together when I called my pastor. But the moment I picked up the phone to call Pete, my thoughts turned on me. *I've let my husband down. I should have tried to raise him from the dead. I hadn't even said, "Live in Jesus' name" the way I'd planned.*

My son had died on my watch.

Pete answered the phone. "Pete, I'm so sorry, he didn't make it," I blurted out. Between sobs, I apologized again and again. Meanwhile, Pete was trying to get his head around what I was saying. All he knew was that something had happened, and it was serious, it was dire. He didn't know about the intubation or the seizure. He hadn't heard the updates from the oncologist. Our last call had simply been a request to pray.

My husband was stunned.

He knew that what I was telling him was true, but it was hard to believe. We'd never entertained this scenario.

For two weeks, we'd been talking about *"When Keagan is healed"*, *"When we're done with this . . ."*

Now all we could do was cry.

Finally, my pastor took the phone from Pete. "We're going to come and get you," he said. "A ministry friend has offered us the use of her plane—and her pilot. Just stay put. We'll be there soon."

◆ ◆ ◆

I hung up the phone as the oncologist came back into the room. "We'll help make arrangements for the body to be transported back to Branson," he said, "but first, we need you to decide if you want an autopsy on Keagan's body."

I knew why my son had died. I didn't need any further explanation, but I agreed. "It's fine," I said. "You can do the autopsy . . ."

Then we began to talk. I knew that one day I was going to have another child, but now I had so many questions. *How did Keagan get leukemia? Is it genetic? If we have another child, could this happen again? Was it something I fed him?*

The oncologist was incredibly kind.

"If we knew what caused it, leukemia wouldn't exist," he said. "We know it could be that there's something in the blood from birth that later goes awry. I don't really have an answer. But if you want to have another baby, have another baby."

We sat and talked together for at least an hour.

Where had the infection come from? Why did it take hold so fast?

"There's nothing you could have done," he reassured me. "There's just nothing."

Eventually, the chaos subsided.

The oncologist began to talk about his experience that day. "I've done this job for a long time," he said. "I'm always the one who offers encouragement and comfort to parents who have just lost their child. But today, I am the one who is being encouraged."

I looked at him, bewildered, as he spoke. "What happened in that waiting room . . . what you did when you prayed and worshiped . . . I've just never seen it before. It was like I saw a picture of what faith is."

He shared with me that his dad had Alzheimer's disease and that he had been praying for him but had never thought about thanking God for answering prayer before he saw the results. He described what he had felt in that waiting room as almost tangible, something he would never forget. "You'll never know what happened on that floor of St Jude's until you get to heaven," he said. "The whole atmosphere changed; people were changed. They could all hear you singing and praising and praying."

We stood up and shook hands. The oncologist had been generous with his time—and his care. Now I needed to return to the Ronald McDonald House and pack up our things, because people were coming to get me to take me home.

The social worker offered to stay with me until my family came. I told her she didn't need to do that, but she insisted. I figured that it was probably protocol not to leave a grieving mother by herself, so I didn't put up much of a fight. She told me she would meet me at the Ronald McDonald House. I didn't care. I just wanted to see my husband.

Turning to walk down the hallway, I determined several things. My mind wasn't exactly at peace, but I had clarity. *I would have another child. I would not allow my faith to be shipwrecked because of what had just taken place. And I would never quit believing that Jesus is the healer.*

As I reached the glass entrance doors, I heard someone calling for me to stop. Turning around, I saw a nurse running toward me. "I just wanted to catch you before you left and tell you that I'm so sorry for your loss," she said. "And I wanted you to know that this whole floor will never be the same after what we experienced today."

She was right. I had felt it too as I sang and prayed. God had been ministering to people in that room. There was a sense of satisfaction inside of me, but at the same time, a deep, deep sense of loss and grief. Walking out of the hospital without Keagan was the loneliest thing I have ever felt. I was numb. I felt like I was leaving something at the hospital. I knew it was my son, but at the same time, I knew he wasn't there. It just felt so unnatural to leave without a little hand in mine.

◆ ◆ ◆

On the airplane were Pete and baby Reece, our pastors, and another friend from church who had offered to drive my car back to Missouri. Everyone was quiet, thinking their own thoughts, trying to come to grips with what had just happened. Pete sat silent as the engine of the plane droned on. Sadness and confusion cluttered his mind. He turned and looked out the window of the plane at the water droplets as they rolled over the top of the wing and vanished out of sight. Inwardly, he was wrestling with what had happened and why. This was not a scenario we had talked about; this was not something he had prepared himself for. Everything had happened around him, yet he wasn't in control of any of it. This was the opposite of what was supposed to be happening.

And then, he heard a quiet voice, still and small, yet powerful and clear: "This changes nothing."

Pete wrestled inwardly. *You're wrong, everything has changed!* He looked at the water drops and reflected on what he had heard.

This changes nothing.

In the quietness of his heart, he knew it was true. *God was still on the throne. He's the same yesterday, today, and forever. With God, there is no shadow of turning. Nothing about Him has changed. His Word is still true, and He is still faithful to His Word.*

"I need to get to Jessica." Pete felt a sense of urgency. "I need to remind her that our son's death had not changed who God is. I need her to know that she must not waver in her faith."

◆ ◆ ◆

I was sitting quietly in a chair at Ronald McDonald House when Pete and our pastors arrived. For the past hour, I'd wept as I packed my son's things into a bag. I'd looked at the computer game I had purchased for him to play while at St. Jude's, realizing that he would never play it. I'd folded his little clothes, knowing he would never wear them again.

I'd thought about what I was going to say to my husband. *He must be so disappointed in me.* The thought couldn't have been further from the truth, but it was hard to shake it. I wondered how Pete was handling things. I wondered if his faith would be shaken.

I stood as I heard their footsteps coming down the hall. My husband immediately grabbed me and hugged me. Our pastors wrapped their arms around us, and for a while, we all just cried. "I'm so sorry, I'm so sorry," I kept saying to Pete. I still felt so guilty that our son had died on my watch.

Pete held me so tight, then he looked at me and said the words that still ring true today: *"This changes nothing."*

I knew what he meant. He was reminding me of what I already knew deep down. Our son may have died, but God was still God. His Word was still true. He was still the mighty healer. When it came to our faith, this changed nothing.

Interlude

Here I am with one child when I used to have two. How can I be a mother to just one? I don't know if I can go back. When Keagan was sick, all I could see was life. All we spoke over him was life. We never envisioned death being a part of this journey, even when he was diagnosed with leukemia. Now there is this intruder into the world we envisioned ourselves in. A thief has come into our most private and secure space, and stolen our most prized possession, our most valuable asset. Death has invaded our home and family. It has pushed its way past the barriers of life that we had set. I feel as though I have been spiritually raped. The intruder has taken something from me that I can never get back.

V
___

Widening the Lens

When Pete announced, "This changes nothing," something in me resonated. We weren't going to change what we believed. We weren't going to stop believing in God's power to heal. God was still our God. We weren't changing our theology. I was in full agreement.

But with that confidence came a barrage of questions.

So why had Keagan died?

Had my faith ultimately failed?

Why did God not keep His end of the bargain?

If Jesus is the Healer, why wasn't Keagan healed?

The questions became more and more far-reaching.

Why do any terrible things happen?

Was there any meaning or purpose to life—or death?

The confusion was mingled with guilt, disappointment . . . and unrelenting grief.

How were we ever to make sense of it all?

In my heart, I knew that the foundations of my faith weren't going to change.

Jesus is the Healer. Scripture testifies to that. He has always healed, and He is still the Healer. Healing is still available today. I wasn't budging on that.

I was also sure of the fact that God is perfect. He doesn't make mistakes, and He is not taken by surprise. He's all-knowing, all-powerful. He didn't look down from heaven and think, "Oh, I didn't see that coming." Whatever took place, I wasn't going to put the blame on God.

I remained convinced that God is good. His intentions and His actions towards us are only good. There is nothing bad or evil in Him.

But of course, that raised other questions.

If God is all-knowing and all-powerful, and if He is always good, why didn't He prevent my son's death? If he does 'all things well', why had things gone so wrong?

Of course, some of my thinking was rather entitled. *If I have a good request, of course He will grant it. I'm His child.* Was it a bad thing to think that way? My children have the key to the house, I reasoned. They can come on in, open the refrigerator, and take whatever they want whenever they want. Maybe a little entitlement comes with simply being a child. I knew God was a good Father, that I was His beloved, and that everything that is His is mine. Surely I was entitled to some entitled thinking! *The very fact that He gave His life for us shows how far He is willing to go for His children,* I reasoned. In my mind, it wasn't unreasonable to expect that, as His children, our every request should be granted. Pete and I weren't asking for anything contradictory to His heart; in fact, we shared His heart! We knew for sure that it was His will that people should live—especially children.

No, I was convinced God was not the problem.

And if that was the case, surely the error or the fault had to lie with me. Had my faith failed in its greatest moment of testing?

The Nature of Faith

When I prayed for my son in that hospital, I just knew my prayers had 'worked'. I could genuinely feel my faith taking charge at that time. But it wasn't 'just' a feeling. Faith was speaking. Faith was listening. Faith was demanding the impossible—only it wasn't impossible in my heart and mind. In my spirit, I never made room for any other outcome, even after my son was pronounced dead.

I remember heading home from the airport and saying to those who were traveling with me in the car, "We need to go to the funeral home together and raise him from the dead." My friends went suddenly quiet. Eventually, one lady gently spoke up, "Jessica, I think we're past that point. That ship has sailed." The other lady agreed, "She's right, I think we're past the point of bringing him back."

These women weren't weak in faith. If anything, they would have been the first to believe for a resurrection miracle. But they also had my best interests at heart. In that moment, they weren't trying to dial back my faith—they were trying to protect me, emotionally and spiritually. They wanted me to do well and to recover. They knew that at some point, the very same faith that had believed for Keagan to live would need to accept that Keagan was gone.

But it took time for my faith to settle down. Even after his funeral, I had no doubt my son could show up alive and well at any time. I remember saying to a friend, "I just feel like he's going to show up on my front porch." I knew it sounded crazy, but I'd exercised great faith, and that faith wasn't easily letting go. My friend understood. "You know, I think your faith is so strong, it just won't quit," she said. ". . . it won't give up. You probably know in your heart that Keagan's not coming back, but there's this thing inside of you that just won't stop believing."

She was right. My thoughts weren't realistic, but neither were they crazy.

I'd been running on pure faith for two solid weeks. Like an athlete who has given it their all in a marathon, when we crossed the finish line, there was nothing else to fall back on. Faith kept surging through my veins. I couldn't fight it. I could only wait for it all to settle down. Thankfully, my friends understood this.

It intrigues me that when Jesus rose from the dead, He chose to linger on earth with His disciples for forty days. Jesus' disciples had been wholeheartedly following Him for three years. All their hopes were in Him. In the weeks leading up to His death, their faith had been stretched beyond what any of them could have foreseen. Imagine the turmoil and inner confusion they would have felt if Jesus had been raised from the dead only to be suddenly whisked away back to heaven. But Jesus knew that their faith needed to settle. Just when His disciples were most prone to disappointment and self-doubt, Jesus came alongside and let them know their next step—they needed to *wait* for the promise of the Father. They needed *time* to process what had happened.

Like the disciples, my faith needed time to settle back to what we had always known to be true.

The Posture of Faith

The very nature of our faith is that God can do what is humanly impossible. But we also know that whenever God works in a miraculous way, it requires human engagement.

In Matthew 8:5-10, we read of a Roman centurion's servant who was at death's door. I could relate to this man's response. He recognized Jesus' authority over death. He knew that there was a spiritual component to what was happening. This man had also put his faith to work. He pleaded with Jesus, "Lord, my servant is lying at the house paralyzed and distressed with intense pains." And Jesus said to him, "I will come and restore him" (Matthew 8:5-13 AMP).

When the centurion sought Jesus, he came with a very clear expectation. He'd heard of what Jesus had done. *Are you kidding me? Jesus has been healing people all around the region! There's no need for this servant to die. I'm going to go get my servant healed—immediately!*

Notice what the centurion didn't do. He didn't talk about how well he had served in the local community or how he had read the entire Torah. He simply brought his request. And when Jesus responds by offering to come to his house and raise his servant, the centurion replies:

> "... *Lord, I am not worthy or fit to have You come under my roof; but only speak the word, and my servant will be cured. For I also am a man subject to authority, with soldiers subject to me. And I say to one, Go, and he goes; and to another Come, and he comes; and to my slave, Do this, and he does it.*"
>
> *Matthew 8:8-9* AMP

When Jesus heard these words, He *marveled at his faith.* "I tell you truly," He said to those who followed Him, "I have not found so much faith as this with anyone, even in Israel" (v. 10).

The centurion knew that the miracle he desired didn't require a physical response—it required a word from the Lord. *Only speak a word, and my servant will be cured.*

A word. Something had caused this man to know that Jesus had the power to heal with a single authoritative word. This centurion understood that, just as those under his authority responded to his every command, sickness and death must respond to the command and authority of Jesus.

When Keagan was fighting for his life, I had operated in the authority I had in Christ, and I had spoken words of life. My outcome was different from what the centurion experienced, but I believe God's response was the same: He *marvels* when He sees us rise in faith.

The Basis of Faith

Even so, something in me felt like I deserved a better outcome. I had put my faith to work.

My belief in God was not based on what I had done or hadn't done. Like the centurion, I wasn't asking something of God based on my worthiness or performance. Yet, I have to admit, a sense of 'I deserved better' was still part of my thinking. All the service to God as youth pastors and worship leaders—was it all for nothing? I felt like even if it wasn't theologically true, I still had a right to have my child healed. I'd served and loved the Lord for years. What was I doing all this for if my faith couldn't even deliver for my family? Besides, I was His daughter! Didn't that justify a better outcome? If the miracle wasn't based on my merit, surely my relationship with God counted for something?

The truth is, in God's economy, nothing is based on merit. We are never going to live this life perfectly.

Pete and I were always 'word of faith' people. We still are. We understand that we are made in the image of God, and that just as He spoke the world into being, our words carry authority—for better and for worse. We know that much of what happens in our lives hinges on what we say.

But we must only say *what our hearts believe*. Our words must align with what we know in our spirit to be true. Even then, there is more to faith than what we can confidently see—or say.

My pastor once said to me, "I used to think faith took care of everything, but if that's the case, the disciple Peter should have drowned as soon as he took his eyes off Jesus and began to doubt and feel afraid. But Jesus stepped in . . ." he observed. "Clearly, not everything hinges on our faith. Some things do, perhaps. But sometimes the outcome is not about us or our faith at all."

My pastor was right. *Some things are just because God allows them. Some things are just because we live in a fallen world. Some things are just because we're human.*

People often get mad at God when things don't go the way they think they should, because the only answer they know is that God is sovereign.

Why did the deer run out in front of the car?
What caused the plane to crash?
Why did the storm close in so quickly?

We run into trouble when our only reply is, "God is in control. God is sovereign." It's an understandable response, but it raises more questions than it answers.

If God is sovereign, why wasn't Keagan healed? For that matter, why didn't God prevent him from getting sick in the first place? And if we go there, then why does anyone get sick at all? Why doesn't God just prevent anything bad at all?

Let's take another look at the faith of the centurion. What was he basing his faith on? Not on the sovereignty of Jesus, but on a recognition of the spiritual realm—that there is more to this world than meets the eye. He knew that we live in a fallen world. He knew the limitations of his humanity. What he was basing his faith on was the *character and attributes of Jesus*. He knew, deep in his heart, two things: that Jesus was good, and that Jesus had the power to heal.

The same is true for us. Our faith can only rest in the sovereignty of God if we understand that the sovereignty of God does not refer to what God does or doesn't *do,* but who God fundamentally *is.* It's referring to the *character* of God.

> *"One thing God has spoken, two things have I heard: That You, O God, are **strong,** and that You, O Lord, are **loving."***
> Psalm 62:11-12

That's exactly the conclusion I came to. Keagan had died, but God was still strong and He was still loving. He hadn't failed on either account. God had remained true to Himself. He was still sovereign.

And we live in a fallen world.

And we are only human.

The Scope of Faith

This fallen world groans under the weight of sin and sorrow. With all our best efforts, we can't right every wrong. The doctors who treated Keagan gave it their all, and ultimately, they reached their limits.

But that doesn't mean that cancer wins the day.

I often think back to when we were fighting for Keagan's life. What was it about our faith that made us adamant that not only our son but *every child on the ward* needed to be healed?

I believe we were sensing God's heart for all humanity. The more I discover God's heart for all of creation, the more convinced I am that there is more to God's purposes than that every individual gets their miracle. God is not willing that *any* should perish.

This leads me to lift my gaze and start believing for something greater. *What if it wasn't just about Keagan's life being saved? What if no child had to suffer from leukemia? What if no one ever had to die from leukemia—or any kind of cancer?*

I believe with all my heart that there's an answer out there, that if there is one doctor who has the medical knowledge and the spiritual depth to seek a cure for leukemia, God in His sovereignty will lead that person to the answer. He's not going to impart that knowledge to me, because I don't possess that level of understanding and knowledge. He'll give it to someone who can understand the medical complexities and physiological processes.

God works through human beings. He's not just 'going to do what He's going to do.' Hanani the seer put it like this:

*"His eyes move to and fro throughout the earth **so that He
may support** those whose heart is completely his."*

2 Chronicles 16:9 AMP

The New King James Version says,

*"The eyes of the Lord run to and fro throughout the whole
earth, **to show Himself strong** on behalf of those whose
heart is loyal to Him."*

If God is going to work powerfully on this earth, He will do it
through *partnership.* He is actively looking for people who share His
heart, not only for their own needs, but for the needs of all people
everywhere.

> *He's got a bigger agenda than my son getting healed
> from cancer.*
> *He wants everyone to be free of cancer.*
> *He's got the **whole world** in His hands.*

These days, I find myself praying bigger prayers. They're less about
me and my particular circumstance. That's the thing about suffering
and loss. It can make us question the sovereignty of God . . . or it can
bring everything into perspective. It helps you realize you're just one
in a million who has lost their child to cancer, or battled their way
through cancer. It helps you grieve, not just for what is happening
in your own life, but for what is happening all across the world. The
whole world is suffering in a multitude of ways.

Sometimes our prayers are very selfish. That's not to say we shouldn't
pray for breakthrough in our situations. As believers, we rise up and
we speak the word of faith in our living rooms, over our finances, in

our college dorms, our workplaces, in the doctor's office. But where faith really kicks in is when we share God's desire for all of humanity to be set free from sin and sickness and sorrow.

I often prayed in tongues for a cure for cancer. The words I need often can't be found in my head, yet as I pray *in the spirit,* I fully believe that God begins moving, looking for ways to bring the person and the cure together for the blessing of many. Instead of diminishing or shaking my faith, my experience of contending for Keagan has only enlarged what I believe God can do. There is a more glorious outcome than one person being saved. It's the whole world being saved! It is God's glory filling all the earth. It is every living being set free from the pain and torment and affliction that we experience.

When we see the bigger picture, we build our faith in what God can do. Think about this: in the eyes of the disciples, the day of Jesus' crucifixion looked like failure. I'm sure they felt the despondency, the confusion, the fear. They felt abandoned—maybe even betrayed. They probably wondered if what they had believed was even real. They'd given their lives to following Jesus for so many years. At His crucifixion, their faith was certainly tested. But it was only a part of the story. They needed to come back to what Jesus had said. *Love would conquer death. The resurrection was still to come.* They needed to remember the bigger picture.

And they needed time. In the forty days Jesus had with His disciples before His ascension, they asked Him, "Will you at this time restore the kingdom to Israel?" (Acts 1:6). Their thoughts were still confined to what they could see. They were focused on Israel. But Jesus widened their perspective:

"You shall receive power when the Holy Spirit has come upon you and you shall be witnesses to me in Jerusalem and in all Judea and to Samaria and to the end of the earth."

Acts 1:8

The ends of the earth were not even on the disciples' radar. They were thinking about their own realm—their own lives and situation. It wasn't until the day of Pentecost that they saw the bigger picture. When the Holy Spirit came upon the believers, they began to see that God's purposes were more expansive and more far-reaching than they had ever realized. The challenge now was to learn to partner with Him for a more expansive outcome.

Hebrews chapter eleven lists some amazing examples of those who lived by faith. Some received their miracle in their lifetime—they saw the dead raised; they experienced deliverance from the mouths of lions. But many of them died still waiting for their miracle. The key is: they all died *in faith.* They saw beyond the here and now. They were assured of the promises of God and kept their suffering in perspective (Hebrews 11:39-40). They knew that eternity lay ahead. It never crossed their mind that God had failed them in their lifetime.

This is the nature of our faith. In the kingdom of God, our own lives and situations matter, but there is always a bigger picture.

VI

When Faith Is Tested

I knew for sure that God wanted Keagan to live, and that He had the power to keep Him alive. So what happened? Well-meaning people would say that my faith was being tested. I have no doubt that is true. But was God the one who was testing my faith?

I can confidently say, "A thousand times, no!"

Why can I say that? Because of the nature of our heavenly Father. Matthew 7:9-11 says,

> *"Which one of you, if his son asks him for bread, will give him a stone? Or if he asks for a fish, will give him a serpent? **If you then, who are evil, know how to give good gifts to your children,** how much more will your Father who is in heaven give good things to those who ask Him!"*

Which one of us would put any child through a test to prove their loyalty to us? It's unthinkable. It's nearly sadistic. Perhaps we think that by bringing God down to our human level, we can make sense of things. Yet our attempt to rationalize suffering and trouble often leads us to meaningless platitudes.

> *God wanted another flower in His garden.*
> *They were too good for this world.*
> *God needed another angel in heaven.*
> *This is just a test that God is giving you.*

God would take a child's life to test me? Really? There is nothing about that statement that aligns with the character and nature of God. God wasn't looking at my life and saying, "Let's float Jessica's boat and see if it has any holes." He wasn't seeking to prove my loyalty. He could see my heart. He already knew whether I was loyal or not, and it didn't make any difference to Him anyway. He loved me before I was loyal. I was, and will always be, His beloved child.

That's not to say my faith wasn't tested. It just wasn't God doing the testing.

It's life's trials that test our faith. *Not God.*

It's the unexpected, unwanted outcomes that test our faith. *Not God.*

The unexpected outcome for the disciple Peter was that he would deny Jesus. Knowing this, Jesus prayed in advance *that his faith would not fail.*

> *"I have prayed for you, **that your faith should not fail**; and when you have returned to Me, strengthen your brethren."*
> *Luke 22:32*

Do you see? Jesus is not testing us to determine whether our faith will fail. He's personally invested in our faith *not* failing!

Amazingly, it seems Jesus has more faith in us than we often have in ourselves. ". . . *when* you have returned to me," He said, as if the possibility that Peter's faith might ultimately fail wasn't even in Jesus's mind.

This indicates something else about the nature of faith and the nature of testing. Our faith is not measured in the moment of crisis. It's in the aftermath that our faith is ultimately tested. Our faith only fails when we walk away from our faith forever.

The Fight of Faith

When Jesus prayed for Peter, He knew that what was coming had the potential to knock him off his game. He predicted Peter would flounder in the moment—He even told him so! It was Peter who was more assured of his faith and loyalty than even Jesus was! "You will deny three times that you know me," Jesus asserts (Luke 22:34). Funnily enough, Jesus doesn't seem the least bit bothered by that fact. What Jesus is concerned about is that Peter's faith is not fundamentally shaken to the point where he walks away for good.

The fight for Peter wasn't in the moment around the fire when his relationship with Jesus was questioned. It was in the aftermath. It was when Peter *felt* like he had failed Jesus that the real fight began. We see this as Peter, filled with thoughts of unworthiness and shame, heads back to his previous occupation. That's when he most needed to fight the fight of faith. He needed to conquer his own thoughts and doubts.

I'm to blame for Jesus' death.
I let Jesus down.
If only I'd stood up for what I knew was right.
I failed in my greatest moment of testing.

Theologically, of course, none of this was true. But emotionally, it certainly felt true.

Peter's mind was conflicted.

He could walk away forever—or he could choose to fight. The apostle Paul would later write:

> *"Fight the good fight of faith, lay hold on eternal life, to which you were also called and have confessed the good confession in the presence of many witnesses."*
>
> *1 Timothy 6:12*

But Peter had no fight left in him. Jesus was dead. He hadn't just failed. He wasn't just ashamed. He was *grieving*. He'd given it his all for the last three years. He'd stayed solid through the ups and downs of Jesus' entire time in ministry. He couldn't shake the thought that when all was said and done, the last words Jesus ever heard him say were, "I never knew the man."

Do you sense his utter disappointment in himself?

He's given up. He's gone back to fishing.

And then Jesus shows up.

You can almost feel Peter's excitement. The love that he had for Jesus when he realized that those words that he spoke, "I don't know the man," weren't going to be the last words Jesus heard from his mouth after all!

All his fear and doubt dissolved in a moment. Peter was so overcome that he plunged into the sea and began swimming with all his might toward Jesus. It never crossed his mind to hide from Jesus or to cower in embarrassment. He knew the heart and character of Jesus. That's why he dove into the water and got to him as quickly as he could—almost like the prodigal son determined to get back to his father. After all the confusion that had been swirling around in his mind, there was a moment of peace. A moment of clarity. The trauma had passed. The fog had lifted.

He wasn't at odds with Jesus after all. He'd just been at odds with himself.

Jesus doesn't even mention what happened in the moment of crisis. He doesn't say, "told you so," or discuss what was going on in that courtyard.

He simply asks, "Simon, do you love me more than these?"

More than the other disciples?

Simon had convinced himself that he had let the others down. He wasn't up for this life of faith.

But Jesus knew Peter's heart. How did Jesus rectify the situation? Simply by allowing Peter to confess that, after all he had been through, he still loved Him.

Picking Ourselves Back Up

Can a person's faith fail? Yes, it can, but not as I once thought. I thought my faith failed when my son didn't get healed, but that was not correct. When faith fails, there is a complete turning away from God. It is deliberately disregarding what the Bible says and going your own way. If my faith had failed, I would not be serving God today. My faith didn't fail. Our situation didn't work out like I thought it should, but my faith didn't fail. Your faith hasn't failed either, or you wouldn't be reading this book, trying to figure out your particular circumstance. You are looking for answers—and that is okay.

But there's another reason Jesus prays that our faith will not fail. Let's look again at Jesus' words to Peter:

> *"Simon, Simon (Peter), listen! Satan has demanded permission to sift (all of) you like grain; but I have prayed (especially) for you (Peter) that your faith (and confidence in me) may not fail."*
>
> Luke 22:31-32 AMP

The disciples had just been arguing among themselves about who would be the greatest—a discussion that would have made Peter feel inadequate, I'm sure. So why did Jesus pray for Peter's faith? I believe that Jesus saw the people who Peter would reach after His resurrection and ascension back to heaven. If Peter's faith failed, it would have had an effect on the entire body of Christ.

The same is true for us. We may have failed in a moment where faith was called for. But a moment of failure does not equal failure. Think of the people God wants you to bless. Whose lives will be touched by your story? Jesus prays that our faith will not fail because there are souls who need the hope and healing we can bring.

Did Peter's faith fail when he denied Jesus three times? No. It was a failure, but we all have failures. The Bible says that after Peter denied Jesus, he went out and wept bitterly. He knew that he had fallen. He remembered Jesus warning him that he would deny Him. But instead of retreating in regret, somehow, Peter pulled himself back up and decided to continue on with Christ. His faith didn't fail.

We cannot allow situations and circumstances to dictate whether we serve God or not. There will be shakings, failures, and upsets along the way, but if we always come back to God, our faith remains. The key to the fight of faith is that when we get knocked down, we get back up. Proverbs 24:16 encourages us with the words: "For a righteous man falls seven times and rises again" (AMP).

We are the getting-up people! As Bishop Dale C. Bronner says, "I only have two positions: I'm either up or I'm getting up!" Don't let anything keep you down too long!

When Faith Gets Shipwrecked

My husband, Pete, and I love going out on Table Rock Lake in our twenty-six-foot deck boat. We've made heaps of family memories there over the years. On a hot day, there's nothing better than fishing for bass and perch, cooking our catch on the Blackstone grill, looking out for mink and otters, and exploring all the coves around the water's edge. One of my favorite things to do is to head out to the middle of the lake, drop the anchor, and dive into the cool, refreshing water. I love to call up my friends midweek and say, "Hey, how about we head out to the lake," and off we go. It's the ultimate day out. But Table Rock Lake is huge—you need to be able to navigate, and you need to stay mindful of all the places you could end up. The shoreline itself stretches seven hundred and forty-four miles!

"You know," Pete reflected to me one day, "if we didn't anchor the boat, we could drift towards all sorts of places, but the funny thing is, boats never seem to drift towards safety."

He was right. When a boat is not anchored, it can end up on a sandbar or run into rocks. There's nearly a hundred percent chance a boat won't just drift by itself into the safety of the dock. The reality is, for a boat to reach the harbor or land back at the dock, it needs to be steered there. Even more so if the boat is on the sea! How many boats have been shipwrecked because the anchor hasn't held when a freak storm arose?

The apostle James used the same analogy for the tongue. He describes our words as a rudder that determines the direction of our lives.

> *"Look also at ships: although they are so large and are driven by fierce winds, they are turned by a very small rudder, wherever the pilot desires. Even so, the tongue is a little member and boasts great things. See how great a forest a little fire kindles!"*
>
> *James 3:4-5*

Even when Keagan died, I found myself speaking in faith. But for many people, a tragedy leaves their faith shipwrecked.

They don't know what to make of it all. They don't know where to drop their anchor. Typically, the words of their mouth become disconnected from what they once believed in their heart.

> *God didn't come through for me.*
> *God abandoned me.*

The more they say it, the more they hear it. And faith comes by hearing. Before long, their faith is in tatters. They've talked themselves out of the things they once held true.

It's a scary thing to be at odds with yourself. We find ourselves drifting in a sea of unknown waters, heading in a direction we never saw ourselves or our lives going.

But not only can our mouths become disconnected from our hearts, they can soon become disconnected from the mooring of God's Word.

I imagine you are reading this and thinking, "But . . . you *did* put God's Word in your mouth. You *did* speak life over your son. You *did* thank God for healing before you saw it with your eyes. *Your son died anyway.*"

I know. But remember, when it comes to my faith, *Keagan's death changes nothing.*

If I allow one situation to determine all my theology, I am in trouble. I have to come back to my moorings. I need to drop anchor in the character and nature of God. I need to use my tongue to steer my ship back to safety.

And so I found myself saying, even in those early, tumultuous days, "I believe God is still a healer. I believe He is still good. I am not going to disregard portions of His Word or begin to pick and choose what I believe because something didn't work out just right in my life. I will not allow my faith to be shipwrecked because of this one incident."

Someone once asked Smith Wigglesworth, "What happens if you pray for someone, and they die anyway?" His response was, "I'll step over their body and pray for the next person." He wasn't trying to be irreverent or uncouth. He was saying that an isolated incident doesn't matter because the Word still holds true. He would keep believing and declaring that if we lay hands on the sick, they will recover.

Did my faith fail? Absolutely not. What I believe, I have spoken. I have not let my mouth run amok. I have not let my words drift into doubt and unbelief. I will never stop praying for the sick. I will not stop exercising my faith for healing just because my son died.

But I am aware that for some people, grief has brought them to the brink of walking away. They're not trying to figure out what happened anymore. They're done. God is no longer in the picture. If that is you, or someone you love, remember that so long as you're still searching, your faith hasn't failed. Don't stay on an island by yourself. Allow God time to help you resolve these things. It takes time to heal. Perhaps this is why the writer of Hebrews says,

> *"Imitate those who through faith **and patience** inherit the promises."*
>
> *Hebrews 6:12*

James also writes about the need for patience.

> *"Let endurance have its perfect result and do a thorough work, so that you may be perfect and completely developed in your faith, lacking in nothing."*
>
> *James 1:4 AMP*

In the aftermath of trauma and suffering, nothing feels sure. It's all foggy, and it's natural to feel tossed and thrown about. It takes time for the storm to settle, the clouds to lift, and for you to be able to think straight once again. You can't walk out too soon, or you'll walk out an angry, disillusioned person. You have to allow time for peace to return. For most people, faith doesn't fail in the middle of the crisis—it fails in the aftermath, when the questions keep coming. *Where was God? Why didn't He come through? Does He even exist?* There are no easy answers to these questions. The resolution doesn't happen overnight. Faith only fails when we give up too soon. But even then, Jesus draws near. And the only question He's asking is this: "Do you still love me?"

It was never a test of our loyalty.

It was a test of our *love*.

And love never fails.

VII

Encountering God

I am so thankful to have been nurtured by pastors who taught us to cling to the promises of God and stand strong in faith. If there's one thing I've learned, it's that we can't afford to ignore our feelings, but neither can we allow them to make the faith call.

There were times in the aftermath of Keagan's death when my feelings took over, but because my root system was strong, my faith wasn't going to be easily torn apart or blown away. In reality, when the funeral and burial were behind us, it was only the root system that sustained me.

And yet down there with the roots, somewhere below the surface, was an issue I couldn't resolve. Whenever I tried to work it out, I remembered my pastors and my husband telling me they hated that I was alone during that time at the hospital. But here's the crazy thing: I never felt alone. God was with me the entire time. I felt His supernatural presence from the moment the nurse walked me across to the waiting room to the moment I saw Keagan's lifeless body. Days later, at his funeral, God was there, strengthening me. I even found myself praying for friends and family who were grieving.

It wasn't until a little after the funeral that I realized how abandoned I felt.

It whittled away at me, and I noticed it, because at times, my thoughts began to get shaky.

Finally, I realized what was going on. I knew that God never leaves us or forsakes us. I'd read it. I'd declared it. I believed it. But the reality was, it *felt* like He had abandoned me.

I felt like God had abandoned me right when I'd needed Him most. Instead of clinging to faith, my mind went to places of unbelief.

> *I did everything I knew to do, and my son didn't live. I prayed, I quoted scripture, I worshiped, I believed, I truly, truly believed God would heal my son. He didn't. He left me in the time of my greatest need. He was tangibly there, touching other people while I prayed and worshiped. He was speaking to the oncologist about thanking God before he saw the answer. He was with a nurse in the waiting room who was experiencing God as I prayed and worshiped. Why didn't He move across the hallway and just touch my son? Why didn't He honor the faith that I was exerting?*

I still don't have an answer to that question. I may never have that answer. But in the months following Keagan's death, the sense of abandonment drove me crazy.

I avoided the conversation for a long time. It affected my prayer life. I didn't want to pray because I couldn't skirt around the topic. Like a relationship issue that's never been addressed, it felt easier to avoid God. But I was left with no choice. I didn't want to accuse God, but I had to be honest with Him.

It came to a head one day when I found myself sitting at my kitchen table, going over and over it all in my mind.

"God, why did you leave me? Why didn't you come through?" I said out loud. "Let's shuck the corn. I feel like you abandoned me!"

I sat with those words hanging in the air.

And then . . . oh, so gently . . . oh, so lovingly, His promise rose within me: "I will never leave you or forsake you."

I'll never forget the gentleness of His response. He didn't say, "Why are you accusing me?" or "Don't you know me better than that?" He gently and lovingly said to my heart, "I will never leave you nor forsake you."

I sat with my words still hanging there, and His words lingering inside of me. Then I said it again: "God, I feel like you abandoned me! I needed you and you weren't there. My son needed you, but you didn't come through! I feel like the devil came and spiritually raped me, and you stood by and did nothing! Where were you? Why didn't you come through?"

Ever so soft and gentle, His words floated up inside of me again: "I will never leave you nor forsake you."

It was the gentleness with which He spoke that finally touched my heart. Now it was up to me.

I either believed it, or I didn't.

If I believed it, I needed to put that issue to bed. And if I didn't, why would I serve a God like that? It was time to choose.

In that moment, I realized I was at a crossroads. I could either choose to believe God's words or I could choose to believe my feelings. It was all or nothing. Either all He says is true, or it's all a lie.

Out loud, I choked out these words: "I *feel* like you abandoned me, but your Word says that you will never leave me nor forsake me, so I choose to believe your words over my feelings."

Then I broke down and cried. Those were hard words to choke out. My feelings were screaming at me that I had been abandoned. It was as if Satan's fiery darts were flying all around me, trying to penetrate my mind and get me to turn from God.

But it was all lies. God had not abandoned me, and He never would.

When I got up from that table, I knew that those feelings wouldn't just go away and leave me alone. Everything in me felt like I had been given a raw deal. But I had made my choice. My feelings weren't going to call the shots anymore. But neither were they going to fester. The Holy Spirit had met me right at the very root issue, and no matter how many times that thought arose, my heart was settled. He'd been there all along.

The thing is, when our feelings push us away from God, we need to make a deliberate choice to press into Him instead. God's got big shoulders. He can handle the difficult conversations. He wants us to bring our accusations to Him. Of course, sometimes we just need to let go. God doesn't want us to hold grudges forever. But neither does He skirt the issue. When we lean into Him, He leans into us. He meets us in the emotional turmoil of the aftermath.

More than that, He sympathizes with His children. He knows how it feels to be abandoned. Think of Jesus' words on the cross: "My God my God, why have you forsaken me?" He's quoting from Psalm 22. He's identifying with a man in despair:

> *"My God, My God, why have You forsaken Me? Why are You so far from helping Me, and from the words of My groaning? O My God, I cry in the daytime, but You do not hear; and in the night season and am not silent."*
>
> *Psalm 22:1,2*

It's so easy to give God the silent treatment because He didn't do what we thought He should do. But God knows that right on the tail of the accusation is a broken heart. We're not going to hurt God's feelings by putting it out there. He's not threatened by our blaming and posturing. He doesn't respond like a human might. He doesn't push back or get defensive. He knows that abandonment and disappointment go hand in hand. He sees our hearts.

For me, the issue felt like God abandoned me in my greatest time of need. For you, it might be different. Perhaps you felt neglected or overlooked in the chaos and turmoil of the moment. Perhaps you felt overloaded or overwhelmed with responsibilities to the point that you couldn't even breathe. Perhaps you felt you 'got it wrong'—that you should have made a different call, but how were you to know?

There comes a point when we need God to show up—not just in the pages of scripture, but right here with us, at whatever 'kitchen table' you find yourself at. In New Testament Greek, the word often used for the Holy Spirit is *paraklētos*—the one who comes alongside. It's not like He's saying, "I'm here, I'm going to walk with you on this path." It's more like you've fallen into a pit, and He's purposefully fallen in with you. He knows what it's like. He knows our sufferings. He recognizes how difficult it's going to be to get out of there. He comes alongside and says, "I'm here to help. Let's get out of this pit together."

There are aspects of our grief that we will never get beyond based on what we 'know' to be true.

The roots are the things that have dug down deep—it's the stuff that holds us to the ground—and if the roots are not doing well, then the whole tree is not going to do well. Sometimes, you need to dig down to the root to figure out what is bothering you, and that's where we need the Holy Spirit's help.

> *"If any man lacks wisdom, let him ask of God, who gives*
> *to all liberally and without reproach, and it will be given*
> *to him."*
>
> *James 1:5 (see also v. 6-8)*

We don't always know what the root issue is. We know there's something, but often we need Him to pinpoint it for us. I encourage you to ask the hard questions. Get real with God, and don't pray some religious prayer. Just be you. Say what you need to say to God. Ask Him to show you what you're missing. Ask Him to show you what needs to be uprooted for you to go ahead and move forward.

God wants your root system to be stable, strong, and healthy. For me, that moment at the table wasn't about general wisdom or generic truth. Yes, it happened to be in scripture. But what I needed at that point in my journey was a personal encounter with God. I needed a personalized response to the issue that was bothering me.

You may have fallen into a different ditch. It's time to turn to the Holy Spirit and say, "How are we going to get out of here?" We don't get to choose how it's going to go. He may give you a word that rises within your spirit, like He did for me. There might be a picture that He places inside of you that suddenly changes your whole perspective. He might invite you to sit on his lap. He might wrap his arms around you, and allow you to tangibly feel his presence with you. You might hear Him sing over you. He might speak to you in a dream.

You don't get to choose how He talks, or how He's going to come to you—but He will come, and He will get to the root of the issue. How will you know it's Him? Because you'll find healing and comfort, and a heart at rest.

VIII

Grief Upon Grief

With the root issue settled, something in me shifted. My beef was no longer with God.

But over time, what I discovered was that there were layers of grief.

For months after the funeral, I just couldn't seem to settle back into my communion with God. I couldn't read the Bible, and I sure couldn't pray. One night, I drove to my church, unlocked the door, walked to the front of the sanctuary, threw myself on the platform, and sobbed. I'd been avoiding spending time with God, but at times like this, it all came flooding out. That night, I told Him how scared I was. *What if it happened again?* I told Him I was terrified of losing my infant son, Reece, or my husband, Pete. My mind played out the scenarios again and again. Me at Reece's funeral. Me at Pete's funeral. I didn't know at the time that these are normal responses, experiences that nearly everyone whose loved one has died an untimely death experiences.

And I was mad. "I'm so mad at you," I blurted out.

At the same exact time that I was angry, I loved Him so deeply. I wasn't about to give up on God. I just needed to make sense of it. My mind was grasping, trying to make sense of this unjust, unholy thing that had happened. I was searching for answers.

It felt so unjust, so unfair. I felt like I'd been taken advantage of. "I've come here to get an answer from you," I cried. "I know that something happened and that it wasn't you, you are perfect, and you are good, so if it wasn't you, then it had to be me. Tell me where I missed it. Tell me what I did wrong!"

I was convinced that Keagan's death had to be because of something I did or didn't do.

That night, the tears just didn't let up. I touched my cheeks. They felt chapped from all the crying. I wiped my eyes—they were swollen and red. It hadn't just been this night—I'd been sobbing for months. At the drop of a hat, I would cry. That's how grief is—it comes on unexpectedly. You can't prepare for it. You can't hold it back. It just is what it is.

I wept for hours that night, and then I was quiet.

If He's going to speak, I need to be still and listen.

All I could hear was the creaking of the metal building I was in.

"What did I do wrong, God?" I asked again. "You have to tell me! You said that if I lacked wisdom, I could come to you, and you would give it to me. So here I am! I'm asking you for wisdom. I have a baby that I still have to raise, and we are going to have another child at some point, so I have to know what I did wrong so that I don't repeat the same mistake with them. Please forgive me for whatever it was that I did. Please tell me so I can learn and move forward."

Again, I waited quietly.

There was nothing. No response from God at all.

I decided to break it down for God. Just one question at a time. Yes or no answer. "Did I not have enough faith?"

No answer.

"Did I not pray enough?"

No answer.

"Was there some sin in my life that kept my prayers from being answered?"

No answer.

"Should I have done something different?" I was getting desperate now.

No answer.

I stayed on the platform for several hours, asking and waiting. Finally, I decided to call it a night. "If it was a lack of faith on my part, please help my unbelief," I prayed. Then I got up, walked out the door, and went home—still with nothing.

Why had God answered my heart's most pressing question at my kitchen table, but now He had nothing to say? It wasn't until years later that I realized the reason I didn't get an answer from God that night was because none of what I was thinking was true.

What I began to understand was that one layer of grief had simply given way to another, and another, until I could barely figure out what it even was that was making me so sad.

The truth is, Keagan's death didn't happen in isolation. My mind went to the week before Keagan was born. My dad had gone to the hospital with a bleeding issue. "It's diverticulitis," the doctors told him. "Are you sure?" my brother asked. "Dad says it feels a lot like the aneurysm he had eight years ago."

"Do you want to diagnose him, or do you want me to?" the doctor replied.

My mom and my brother kept me updated on the situation, but there was nothing I could do. My contractions had already started. I was going to give birth any moment. "It's okay," they assured me. "Stay home. It's not urgent."

But I knew something was wrong. The doctors hadn't figured it out. My dad had been to see me three months earlier, and he'd been having the bleeds then. *Was it really diverticulitis?* Dad had already had surgery, and it hadn't improved.

When Dad asked to see a doctor again, he was told that the doctors had all left for the 4th July holiday. At that point, he demanded to be moved to another hospital.

By the time the medics wheeled my dad out of the ambulance and got him admitted into another hospital, my dad was in bad shape. The doctors took one look. "It's the aneurysm," they said, and immediately took him into surgery.

The next thing I got was a call to say he didn't make it.

Three days later, Keagan was born. I was two weeks past my due date, Keagan was a ten-pound baby, and to all our surprise, he needed to be delivered by C-section.

"I can't leave the hospital for a few more days," I said to my mom. "I can't even walk. Go ahead and have the funeral." The funeral home director knew our family well and kindly offered to keep the casket unsealed until I could get there. I'd miss the funeral, but at least I could see his body, say goodbye, and be there when he was buried.

Still, on the day I was finally discharged, my doctor expressed his concern. He knew my hormones were still adjusting, I'd just had major surgery, this was our first baby, and the burial was being held two hours away from where I was.

Pete picked me and our baby son up from the hospital, and we drove straight to the funeral home. It was only after my dad's burial that I realized he was the glue that held our family together. With him no longer with us, our family began disintegrating. Mom became lost in her own grief, my younger brother had moved to another state to be 'used by God', and later, my other brother and my mother moved away as well.

Years later, I found my son Reece crying. "Why doesn't Grandma love me?" he wanted to know. "Why doesn't she want to see me?"

Pete's mom died when Reece was three. One day, I heard Reece say to an older lady at our church, "Will you be my grandma?" I didn't realize he needed grandparents as much as he did.

Pete and I were effectively left with no connection to aunts or uncles, cousins or even parents, while we raised our young family.

When my mother told me she was moving to Montana, I cried and cried. "My kids aren't even going to know you," I told her, but she brushed it off. The reality was, she'd only visited once in all those years.

Even when Keagan died, my mother wasn't sure she wanted to come to the funeral. In the end, my pastor's wife called her and said the church was going to arrange flights for her and my brother to be there. "Jessica needs you," she said. "This is a horrible time for her. Her family needs to be around her."

In the end, my mom agreed to come, but reluctantly. As soon as the funeral was over, my two brothers left with my mom to visit some old friends they hadn't seen in years.

Sometime after, I was crying on the phone, processing what I was going through out loud to my mom. "Well, I don't know," she said to me. "God rained down judgment on people in the Bible."

"You seriously think God took my son to teach me a lesson?" I asked. My mom was quiet. "I take it from your silence that's what you're saying," I told her. "But just so you know, you're wrong."

It was the last time we discussed Keagan's death. I made up my mind there and then that I was not going to give my mom permission to speak into my life on that topic anymore.

It wasn't until some time after my night of railing at God in the church sanctuary that I realized, *it wasn't God who abandoned me; it was my family.*

It felt like I was mad at God, but in fact, I was mad at my mom.

I'd never felt unloved by my mom—until I was an adult. When I needed her most, she wasn't there. More than that, she turned on me. There was no comfort. No compassion. No reassurance. I thought back to all the times my mom and I would talk for hours about faith and God. My mom was a wealth of knowledge about bible stories. But since she moved away, it was as if she became a different person. Her whole perception of God changed, and we couldn't agree on things any longer.

It was grief on top of grief.

God saw the grief, but He also saw the *cumulative* grief. And He cared. It wasn't about what I had or hadn't done. It had nothing to do with the questions I'd been asking God. Finally, He'd got to the heart of the matter. It wasn't God who had abandoned me. It was my family.

It was healing for me to realize that God had already filled the hole my family had left. It spoke volumes to my heart that my pastor's wife had reached out to my mom before Keagan's funeral. I remembered the friends who cried with me as if they'd lost their own child.

The people from our church had become our family. God hadn't left us alone. He shared in the disappointment. He understood the unmet desires and expectations of my heart. We'd been surrounded by people who had loved us the way I'd needed my family to love us. And He ministered to us through them.

IX

Opening the Floodgates

Getting the abandonment issue in my heart resolved came as a great relief. But over time, I longed to get back into the disciplines and habits that had always undergirded my life. For a long time, I'd stood in faith on the Word of God, declared promises over my life, shared scriptures with other people . . . but when I tried to read the scriptures, it all fell flat.

The truth is, in difficult times, reading the scriptures can seem dry and empty. I read the words on the page, but they were *just* words on a page. For the first time in my life, the Bible felt impersonal.

I remember at one point feeling like I needed some hope. I began to read scriptures on hope, but it didn't do the trick. It made me question more, wonder more. That's okay, of course—God doesn't mind our questions and wonderings. But it was as if the scriptures were mocking me. Sometimes I would read the verse, "Hope does not disappoint," then I'd stop reading and cry and tell the Lord, ". . . but I am disappointed!" I tried to rationalize it. "I guess it's talking about the blessed hope, our hope of eternity," but the attempt fell flat. It wasn't hitting home.

I knew I needed to keep reading the Bible even if it sometimes felt like walking through a desert. I looked up scriptures and searched things out, even when it felt empty. I'd ignore my feelings and choose to read, simply because God's Word is true. It's much like prayer. Sometimes prayer can feel dry, barren or fruitless, but as believers, we pray anyway because we know God hears us. In fact, it's right there in those dry places that God tends to show up. Moses was on the back side of the desert tending his father-in-law's sheep when all of a sudden, he saw a burning bush and heard God telling him to take off his shoes because he was standing on holy ground. It wasn't the desert place that made it holy; it was God's presence that made it holy. From that point on, Moses had a burning in his heart. He had direction. It was out of that encounter with God that Moses went and confronted Pharaoh.

The two disciples on the road to Emmaus were also in a dry place. Only days earlier, Jesus had died, and now His body had been taken. They were feeling heartbroken and hopeless. Things were getting crazy. They had hoped it was Jesus who would redeem Israel and set their nation free. Now their hopes were dashed. Jesus was dead. Then, as they walked along that desert road, Jesus showed up. At first, they didn't recognize Him. That's what heartbreak can do. It can cloud our eyes. But Jesus wasn't in a hurry. Gently, He came alongside them, walked with them, listened to their questions, and as He began to show them from Moses through the prophets, God's plan and how it all pointed to Jesus, their hearts burned within them. "Stay with us," they asked, and as He broke bread with them, their eyes were opened and they realized who He was. Jesus vanished from their sight and was suddenly gone, but for the disciples, everything had shifted. In one encounter with Jesus, their hope was restored! Running back to the other disciples, they couldn't wait to share the news with them.

When we find ourselves in a dry place, we need to remember that spiritual disciplines such as reading the Bible and prayer can take us so far, but there comes a point where we need Jesus to show up. It's His presence that brings the scriptures to life and makes them feel very real and personal.

We don't need to seek an experience as such; we seek God Himself. And we seek answers. In our confusion and despair, we don't run away from Him, we run to Him! We continue to read the scriptures and pray, but we also call out to Him and tell Him, "I need you. I can't do this without you. What do you want to say to me? What do you want me to know?"

And then we take time to just listen. We choose to be still and know that He is God. There's no formula. Whenever we are real with God, it causes Him to be real back. He is near to the broken-hearted. I recall God appearing to me far more often when I was at my lowest than when I was at a high point in life or when I was feeling victorious. The scripture is true:

> "The Lord is close to the brokenhearted and saves those
> who are crushed in spirit."
>
> Psalm 34:18

When we feel like retreating, Jesus draws near. Think of Peter after he denied the Lord. He was out fishing when he noticed Jesus had lit a fire on the beach and was cooking fish for breakfast. No wonder Peter dove into the water and swam to get to Him!

It's the same with us. When we are at our lowest, sometimes not even attuned to His presence, Jesus draws near. He steps into our familiar lives. We can't manufacture it. We must simply open our hearts and be ready for an encounter with God.

◆ ◆ ◆

One night, a few months after Keagan had passed away, I lay in bed trying to go to sleep, but grief was consuming me. My husband was sound asleep next to me, but my thoughts were on a loop: *If God is all-powerful, why isn't my kid here?*

I knew that if I didn't resolve this question, my mind could get stuck in this loop for a very long time. I might never get peace. I knew He was the only one with the answer. If the issue was ever going to be settled, it needed to come from Him.

Then, in the darkness, I sensed God drawing near. It reminded me of Genesis 1:2: "The spirit of God was hovering over the face of the deep . . . *and then God spoke.*"

I believed God was calling me to come and talk to Him, but I wanted to avoid the conversation. I don't know why, exactly, except that when someone has hurt you, you just tend to avoid them. Eventually, I knew the topic had to be confronted.

I wanted to rationalize my thoughts, but instead of walking to the kitchen table and opening my Bible, something drew me towards

Keagan's room. I hadn't been back in there since he died, other than to put something back on the dresser or in his closet.

The door was closed. I opened it and walked in. His little boy scent was still on his pillow. The bed he'd slept in wasn't made, the blankets were piled on it as if he had just woken up and left them there. The toys he'd played with were scattered around the floor. Dresser drawers were still open from when we had rushed into his room to pack for the hospital stay. I went over to Keagan's bed, knelt down on the floor, and began to cry. I missed him so much.

As I gathered myself together, I began to pray in tongues because I just didn't know what to say in English. Then an incredible boldness overtook me, and I blurted out:

> *"Okay, God, I want my kid back. I know you didn't take him, and I am sure not blaming you. I know that Satan came to kill, steal and destroy, but I also know that you came to bring life and life to the fullest! I know you have received Keagan. I know who you are! I'm not some mom who has never known you. I know what you are capable of. I want my son back! I know he's been dead a little while, but I know you are the God who raised Lazarus from the dead after four days. This is nothing for you. I know you are well able to do this, and as your daughter, as your child, I am calling on you to raise my son out of that graveyard and transport him to me and put him on my front porch. I'm not stupid. I know who you are! You are all-powerful. You are life!"*

Again, I was met with silence. It was the last time I ever prayed that prayer.

I don't know if what happened next was a vision, because I didn't see it with my eyes. I don't even know if my eyes were open or closed, but the image was real. Jesus was sitting in a chair over by the window, and Keagan was sitting on His lap, his head resting on Jesus' chest.

"I want my son back," I said to Jesus. "I know who you are . . ." I said the words again and again, but every time I said, "I want my son back," Keagan turned his face further into Jesus' chest. "Come on, I know you are well able," I kept saying, "Your Word says that nothing is impossible for him who believes. Well, I believe! I believe you are more than able to make this happen."

I kept begging, while Jesus just sat there, holding my son. I noticed that the more I talked, the more Keagan turned his head toward Jesus and wouldn't look at me.

Slowly, I began to realize that what I was asking for wasn't just between Jesus and me. Keagan had a say in this as well. Seeing Keagan bury his face in Jesus' chest and arms, a strange truth began to dawn on me: *My son didn't want to come back.*

Suddenly, everything made sense. *Why would anyone want to come back to earth after being physically with Jesus?* It was my son making this choice, not me, and not Jesus.

I began to sob. "Jesus, I miss him so much," I cried. "It's not even the physical stuff like hugging him or kissing him. There are things we had been doing together that feel incomplete. We were working on his ABCs, and I didn't get to finish doing that with him. I miss talking to him and hearing him tell me stories and sharing what had happened each day. I miss laughing with him and going places with him. It's just the relationship that I miss."

Then I said something crazy. I said, "But you don't understand, Jesus. You don't get it because you never got married and had kids while you were here on this earth. You don't know what it's like. As a parent, kids are connected to our heart, and you wouldn't understand that."

Telling Jesus He doesn't understand is just crazy, I suppose, but that's how it felt. I was being real and honest with Him. I felt like I was the only one in the world who had ever experienced pain or sadness.

Up to this point, Jesus hadn't said anything. He just sat there with my son's face buried into his arm. Finally, He spoke. "I do understand," He said. "I understand feeling the separation and missing talking to him. I do have children. They are all over the world, and I don't feel like I'm finished with them either. I want to teach them the ABCs of faith. I want to bring them close and hear about their day. I want to bless them and provide for them, but they just don't know that this kind of relationship is available."

Suddenly, I realized that how I felt about my son was how Jesus feels about all of us. It was eye-opening in the most endearing kind of way. In that moment, I loved Him more than ever. I'd felt the grief in His heart—and He knew the grief in mine.

With that revelation, the floodgates opened. As I sobbed, it was as if my heart opened to His heart and we were grieving together—not just for my son, but for all those who were far from Him. "I need you to go and tell them," Jesus said. "I need you to tell them that I miss them, and I love them, and I want to have a close relationship with them—and when you are done, I will restore your relationship with you and your son." It wasn't a bribe, it was a promise for the future. It was also the best offer I had all day!

In my heart, I agreed—and with that, there was an acknowledgement that my son wasn't coming back. It was a bittersweet moment. I would be reunited with my son at some point, but for now, I had work to do.

◆ ◆ ◆

We often come to the scriptures looking for one-size-fits-all truths. But in my experience, it took a personal encounter with Jesus to move beyond the stagnation and confusion. Just like the disciples on the road to Emmaus, my hope had been restored. I was no longer questioning God's sovereignty or His goodness. I wasn't bargaining with Him anymore. Jesus had come and fallen into the pit with me. He not only saw my despair and hurt, but He had shared His heart with me. We understood each other's grief.

When I walked back into the bedroom, Pete was still lying in bed, asleep. But for me, everything had just changed. This was more than just an emotional response. My spirit had grabbed hold of the revelation God had given me, and for the first time on this journey, I began to see the bigger picture. My life had purpose. Beyond my son's death, there was hope.

X

Run the Race

In the months following Keagan's death, Pete and I had held onto the statement, "This changes nothing." It gave us something to grasp in the turmoil. More importantly, it had held us together as a couple.

On the surface, I had struggled with Keagan's death more than Pete did. Did that mean Pete didn't love Keagan as much as I did? I can understand now why someone might presume that. Pete and I talked about Keagan and that situation a lot. Even so, there was much about Pete's grief I didn't pick up on at the time.

My struggle was palpable, even visible. You could see it on my face; it came out of my mouth; I could cry at the drop of a hat. But for Pete, the waters had run deep. He'd accepted what had happened and the grief was not easily seen, but it was there. Keagan's death had also raised questions for Pete that affected him on a heart level. By now, I'd already had two significant encounters with God, both of which had the potential to move me a long way forward in the grief process. Pete, on the other hand, was 'steady as she goes'.

One day, Pete turned to me and said, "Hey, I've written a song." That surprised me. Pete had written a few melodies and songs when he was younger. But this was different. This wasn't a song to share with other people or sing at church. I recognized immediately that this was his way of processing his feelings around Keagan's death. "Will you sing it for me?" I asked. When Pete sang it for me, it didn't move me or speak to me in any particular way. I couldn't say, "Wow, that was a beautiful song!" What it did show me was how much I loved my husband.

But one Sunday, Pete received a full-blown vision. Pete is a 'people watcher'—he notices the most minor details about everything—so we always sat in the front row in church, just to minimize distraction! That day, as he dismissed the service, our pastor asked the whole congregation to stand. Later, Pete told me what happened in that moment:

> *"As I stood up, the church and everything in it completely disappeared. You and I were on a black running track in a huge arena. In front of us, the lanes were all marked out in white paint. We were positioned as if about to compete in a race. The stands were packed with people. As we were preparing to take our positions at the blocks, I was looking around the sea of faces. And then I saw Keagan, way at the top of the stands."*

Pete reminded me, "You know how we used to pick Keagan up from daycare? We'd walk into the room and he wouldn't see us at first, but then he'd turn and see us and his eyes would light up. His whole face brightened, and he'd give us the biggest smile and run to us? That is kind of what happened."

> *"The moment he made eye contact with us from up in the stands, his face lit up! We couldn't hear him, but we saw him mouth the words in a cheer, 'MOM! DAD!' Then all of a sudden, the stadium and its crowds were gone, and I was back in the church."*

As the pastor was praying over the congregation, a scripture floated into Pete's mind:

> *"Therefore we also, since we are surrounded by so great a cloud of witnesses, let us lay aside every weight, and the sin which so easily ensnares us, and let us run with endurance the race that is set before us, looking unto Jesus, the author and finisher of our faith, who for the joy that was set before Him endured the cross, despising the shame, and has sat down at the right hand of the throne of God."*
>
> *Hebrews 12:1-2*

The service was over. The congregation was beginning to leave. Pete stood there for a moment, then turned to me and shared what he had just seen. "Jess, we have to run!" he said. "We can't sit down, we can't give up, we can't quit. We have to *run* this race . . . not just jog, but run!" Pete was energized as he spoke:

> *"When I get to heaven, I want to hear Jesus say, 'Well done, good and faithful servant.' But I also want to run this race in a way that gets my son on his feet in the grandstands of heaven and causes him to shout out,*

'MOM! DAD!' and cheer us on. I don't want him to look at me when this life is over and say, 'Why didn't you run? Why did you quit? Why did you sit down? I was cheering for you . . . why didn't you run?' I want him to be able to say, 'Dad, I saw when you led that young person to Christ. I cheered with all of heaven when he was born again. I cheered when you preached that message and people's lives were changed. I cheered when I saw you do things that no one else saw you do . . . I was cheering you on the whole time.'"

I cannot put into words how that vision put the wind back into our sails. It was the moment that shifted the whole perspective for Pete. It was also the moment I felt the urge to get up and keep going. I couldn't stay sitting down on the path of life. I couldn't call in sick and just stay home and cry all day. The truth was, life was moving forward, but mine had stopped. My heart and mind were in a better place, but another part of me didn't even want to move on—I wanted to just sit there and set up camp in the moment when Keagan was last with me. But Keagan wasn't camping there—he was up on his feet, cheering us on! Even though my legs were weary, and it sometimes felt like my heart couldn't keep beating, I had to get up and *run*.

Our pastors encouraged us:

"You need to grieve. You need to cry. But there's this thing about grief, that it can hang on and on. It can keep you stuck, and depression stems from that. It's not that we're trying to hurry you along. But we are cautioning you

*as we walk the road of grief that this can happen. You
don't want to get stuck here."*

And so I determined that when I was sad, I was going to cry, but
then I was going to wipe my face and get up and get on with my day.
I was going to make dinner and go to work. I'm a verbal processor,
so when people asked how I was doing, I told them. But I also knew
that I wasn't going to stay grieving forever. One vision, one moment
of revelation, had shifted everything.

"Keagan's more alive now than he's ever been," one friend reminded
me—and he was right. I had seen Keagan burying his face into Jesus'
shoulder. But Pete had seen him up on his feet, full of passion, full
of excitement, actively engaged in my life! My son was in the great
cloud of witnesses. What do witnesses do? They witness events. They
see things! Keagan was watching! I needed to run well.

One day, I was out on a walk, earbuds in my ears, listening to
music, when all of a sudden, I got a keen awareness that my son was
very proud of what I was doing. You see, I have a thing for food. I
like cooking. I enjoy food. Watching what I eat doesn't come easily.
But still, I was trying to lose weight. Keagan saw all that, and he was
cheering me on.

The same thing happened when his sister was born. I was sitting
there in the hospital bed holding our tiny daughter, and I just knew:
He can see her. He knows he has a sister.

The funny thing is, I never felt like Keagan saw us eating dinner
or doing the day-to-day things of life. He saw the moments that
mattered. The eternal moments, the moments that meant we were
moving forward—like the birth of his sister. That moment affected him.

Even as I write this book, I have this sense that my son is cheering me on. This is his story as much as it is mine, only he can see a little further than I can. He can see the results. "Mom! This is helping someone today! Keep writing!" he tells me. "Write through the tears and write through the hard things. Write, Mom! Someone will read this and receive healing. Someone will read this and have the courage to run their race!"

There's something special about generations of people cheering each other on. I think of my great-great-grandfather and the prayers he prayed that connect me to him. I think of the handwritten love letters he wrote to my great-great-grandmother: "You know, we don't have much money but we have each other and we have Jesus." It's the sweetest love story to me. My great-great-grandparents died forty-eight hours apart. They're together now, and they're probably with my son, watching as their great-great-granddaughter and her husband pick themselves up off the track and decide to *run!* Are they all in the same section of the stands, just cheering me on?

My grandmother compiled a booklet of family stories. She tells my great-grandfather's testimony, how he clapped his hands for joy at the moment of salvation. She writes about how he ran a general store and how God convicted him about selling and smoking tobacco. She wrote about his baptism in the Holy Ghost and how he prayed five times a day for his children, his grandchildren, and his great-grandchildren. He prayed for me!

My great-grandfather wrote a poem called "This home of mine." It's about how home is not about everything matching or being perfect. It's about simple things, like the rain falling on the tin roof and the pattering of little feet. Today, it hangs on the wall of my home. When

I see it, I feel so connected to my great-grandfather, even though I never knew him. This man got it. Home isn't about how big our house is. It's about family. Now, he's seeing the fruit of his prayers. What a reward! We may not see all our prayers come to pass, but one day we will get to peek through the veil and see God's promises being fulfilled in our children, and our children's children, and in all the generations that follow.

I find it no surprise, therefore, that in light of Pete's vision, both of our children ran cross country—in high school and junior high, both Reece and Charis competed at state level in their division. My nephew (who was named after Keagan) also runs cross country. He isn't just a mediocre runner, either. He received a scholarship to run in college. These kids didn't just run ... *they ran well.*

Running well is a theme that has become embedded in our family's DNA. My son, Reece, attended a Bible-based gap year program before going to college. At the end of the year, each graduate had to pick a 'life verse'. Sure enough, Reece picked Hebrews 12:1, not because we told or encouraged him to—he was only ten months old when Keagan died; he doesn't even remember him—but because there is a mandate on our family to *run the race.* Today, Reece feels called to ministry. My daughter Charis is only seventeen right now, but she also has developed a gift in speaking and preaching, especially to young people.

Whatever we are called to do, we must not allow grief to slow us down or cause us to quit. There is a cloud of witnesses cheering us on! Don't allow your current circumstances to knock you out of your race. Get up, friend! Run! There will be a finish line, and when you cross it, the grandstands of heaven will be full of people ready to greet you and congratulate you for a race well run. Run even though your sides hurt. Run even though you can't feel your legs. Push yourself to keep going, and allow the wind of the Spirit of God to refresh you as you run. Remember that Jesus has also run the race. He is there too, cheering us on!

His grace is sufficient. His strength is made perfect in weakness. Sometimes we just have to encourage ourselves and tell ourselves what we really do believe. Sometimes we say it with tears streaming down our faces. Sometimes we say it in the face of the enemy's taunts. But as we confess these truths, God will help us and meet us where we are.

I am not alone, and you are not alone. We are running this race together. Today, I am running up beside you and telling you to keep running! Run your race and endure! I know you are hurting, but keep running. There is a prize ahead of you. Don't stop, don't quit—come on, I'll run with you! We can do this together. Stay with me, run beside me. Regulate your breathing. Keep your eyes up and looking ahead. Let's run well, and let's finish well.

XI

Fighting the Fear

Pete's vision infused fresh life into our weary souls. But then, somewhere along the track, fear kicked in. For me, it was constant, a barrage of fear that never let up. My mind couldn't shake the thought: *If death can touch a four-year-old boy, nothing's off limits.*

I was afraid we could lose another child. I was afraid our good friends, the pastors who had walked through this with us, would die. I was afraid I would die and leave my children without a mother, my husband without a spouse. I didn't want anyone to grieve like I had been grieving.

My thoughts were consumed with the possibility of death.

I wasn't going crazy. This was a natural human response. For years, I'd been able to brush aside my fears, or spiritualize them: *Well, God will take care of me.* But this was different. In the words of C.S. Lewis, "No one ever told me that grief felt so like fear."

I knew that fear was not of God. This felt like an attack. For six to nine months, the fear was relentless. *Reece could die. My husband could die. I could die.* It never let up. What a contrast to the apostle Paul, who wrote, "To live is Christ and to die is gain" (Philippians 1:21).

I know it is a natural response to face our own mortality when someone passes, but this was different. I wasn't just thinking about death. Fear took over my thoughts and almost ran them daily. Before Keagan's death, I was bold. My college roommate described me as 'fearless' the moment we met. Sure, I had natural fears, like the fear of heights. Roller coasters and parachuting certainly aren't my hobbies. But I had confidence that with God, nothing was impossible for me. Now I was dealing with fear all day long, and it was paralyzing.

It started with questions: *What if Pete dies? What if Reece dies? What if I die? What if my best friend dies?* Very soon, the questions turned into scenarios in my mind. I found myself playing them out one by one, trying to make a plan for how I would deal with each one. It was as if I was preparing for everyone around me to die, or for everyone who needed me to cope if I died.

I thought of Reece dying and pictured how horrible that would be. I had already lost one son, and now (in my fearful mind) I had lost my second son. I could already see everyone rallying around me again, only this time, the grief would take me out. I saw myself not able to get out of bed. I saw myself becoming bitter and hateful toward people. Tears would just run down my face, and before I knew it, I was sobbing and mourning the death of Reece, who was alive and well and thriving.

My thoughts soon gained a life of their own. The more I indulged them, the more fantastic the storyline became. At first, I beat myself up for allowing my thoughts to run wild. *Snap out of it,* I told myself. *You're thinking crazy thoughts. What are you doing?*

Funnily enough, my mind wasn't going down these paths when I was at work. At work, I had to stay focused on my job and what I was doing. It was in the quiet times when I was at home by myself, at night when I was going to sleep, in the mornings in the shower, or when I was driving in the car. Whenever my thoughts and I were alone together, I was overwhelmed by fear.

One weekend, I was at home doing a load of laundry. I'd been crying a lot that day. It started out as grieving for Keagan. But as I put the clothes into the dryer, I began imagining Pete dying. I thought about how much everyone loved him (which they do . . . he is a great guy!) and how devastating his death would be to everyone. I imagined his friends telling stories about him, stories that would make us all laugh, then cry because we loved him so much. I imagined how empty I would feel, how I wouldn't have anyone to talk to at the end of each day. I thought about how I am a verbal processor, and suddenly, my thoughts took off. *How would I ever process anything correctly again? How would I manage financially? I would have to work until I died. I would have to sell our home and live in a tiny apartment. How would I raise Reece without a father? How would I manage to pay for college or even T-ball?*

My mind was running rampant, to the point where I could see my husband's casket and all the flowers at his funeral. Breaking down in front of the dryer, I was sobbing over the loss of my husband.

Suddenly, I saw how ridiculous this had become. If someone had asked why I was crying, what would I say? "I'm imagining my husband dead?!" The whole thing was crazy.

Standing up, I said to myself out loud, "What are you doing? He's not dead! He's alive. Stop this crazy thinking right now! You're losing it!"

It was time to place a bit in the mouth of these wild horses. I got up off the floor and walked back into the living room, feeling ashamed of myself. *Why had I allowed my thoughts to go there again?* This had been happening a lot. *Why was I allowing my mind to run my emotions?*

It's hard in these moments to distinguish between what is grief, and what is our thought life running amok. Grieving the loss of Keagan was one thing, but grieving the loss of people who were still very much alive? That was totally different.

I needed to do something. I needed to change my thoughts, *but how?* By the time they were in my mind, they were already spinning their own graphic story. I remembered a down-to-earth Texan preacher once saying, "Negative thoughts are like birds, you can't keep them from flying around your head, but you can keep them from building a nest in your hair."

It was time to evict the birds that had taken up residence in my head. *But how?* I decided this was war. I needed to *combat* what was going on in my mind. 2 Corinthians 10:3-6 says:

> *"For though we walk in the flesh, we do not war according to the flesh. For the weapons of our warfare are not carnal but mighty in God . . . for casting down arguments and every high thing that exalts itself against the knowledge of God, **bringing every thought into captivity** to the obedience of Christ."*

I knew the character of God: *God is good. God is love. God has a future and a plan for us. He has not given us a spirit of fear, but of power and love and a sound mind.* Anything that exalted itself above what I knew of God needed to be taken captive.

The pictures that had taken up residence in my mind were very vivid. *The caskets. The flowers. The sobbing friends.* It was all very convincing . . . and depressing. None of it was life-giving. I needed to take my imagination captive and put it to work in a life-giving way. Philippians 4:8 holds the key:

> *"Finally, brethren, whatever things are true, whatever things are noble, whatever things are just, whatever things are pure, whatever things are lovely, whatever things are of good report, if there is any virtue and if there is anything praiseworthy—**meditate on these things.**"*

Good report. Praiseworthy. Those words resonated inside of me. Pete dying, Reece dying—that was a bad report. It wasn't praiseworthy. I needed to replace those pictures, and I needed to be deliberate about it.

What would be a good report? I asked myself. *Pete living a long life.* That would be a good report. *Reece, living out his life and living for God.* That would be a good report; it would be praiseworthy.

I began to re-create each scenario in my mind. I imagined myself and Pete growing old together. I imagined a family picture with the two of us sitting in chairs, and our children and grandchildren and great-grandchildren standing around us. I imagined all the generations serving God, attending church, bearing witness to Christ. I visualized the smiles on our faces and the joy and laughter in that group of people that surrounded us. I saw us sharing stories and laughing around the table. I imagined us attending doctor's visits and coming home with a good report. I pictured us all praising God together for His goodness toward us.

It was just a beginning, but something had shifted. The birds were leaving the nest.

❖ ❖ ❖

I have learned that it's nearly impossible to combat a thought with a thought. To round up our reckless thoughts and bring them into submission, we need to use our words. With a new picture in my mind, I began pacing the house and declaring a new reality: "I refuse to live in fear. God has not given me a spirit of fear, but of power, love and a sound mind. I don't have crazy thoughts. I have God-thoughts."

Then I would say, "I see myself living to be a good old age—and Pete, right there beside me. I see our children and our children's children and their children, all gathered around us. I see us all serving God. I see us all happy and fulfilled, living a beautiful life. I see us full of joy, full of peace, full of love for one another."

As I paced that floor and declared the goodness of God over our lives, joy and hope entered my heart. Fear kept trying to dominate, but it was on the losing side. Even so, I can't emphasize enough how persistent I needed to be. The thoughts were literally a barrage. They didn't let up easily or quickly. It was exhausting. But I had a strategy, and it was bringing joy and life and light to my future. Whenever I had thoughts of death and fear, I'd turn around and audibly describe what my heart had seen. This went on for a period of several months—at first, multiple times a day, then it began to lessen to every other day, and then, once or twice a week.

Fear was lifting. I felt like I was on top of it—I still had to be diligent, but a few months down the track, fear wasn't dominating anymore. And then, I had a dream that showed me a more sinister side to what I was dealing with. Until now, I had reclaimed the territory in my mind. But in my dream, I saw that I was also dealing with a *literal spirit of fear.*

In my dream, I was lying on my side in bed, looking across the room, when suddenly, a dark little head poked out from behind the bathroom door, then darted back in. Fear gripped me all over. My body instantly went stiff. I couldn't move. I knew it was a demon. It was very small in stature, dark like a shadow, and it had very monkey-like features. It wasn't tall and imposing. It was impish. Like my thoughts, it was hard to pin down. Paralyzed with fear, I watched the demon hop onto my bed, then bounce around between the bed and the wall.

In my dream, I began to take authority over the spirit that had been tormenting me. My poor husband, lying on the other side of the bed, woke up to hear me screaming, "In the name of Jesus, you demon of fear, I resist you! The Bible says if I resist you, you have to flee, so *go now* in Jesus' name!"

Pete looked at me groggily. "Whaaaaattt?" he said.

"Pray in the Holy Ghost right now!" I told him. Pete started praying while I kept declaring that I would not be tormented by a little impish devil.

What happened that night is the most vivid encounter with evil I've ever had. But here's the beautiful thing: The spirit of fear had no control over me; I was in full control of it. If I had lain there stiff and silent, it might have tormented me even more. Instead, I took authority over it. I wasn't afraid. It was like a vicious animal that just needed to be restrained. It wasn't all-powerful. It wasn't even threatening. It was just a pesky little imp that wouldn't let up unless I told it where to go.

From that night on, I have never been harassed by fear. I have had fearful thoughts, but like the birds flying over my head, they soon pass and go on their way. They have no place to land in my life. That's what it looks like to stand in the authority we have in Christ.

For months, I had been tormented by the fear of death. But Hebrews 2:14-15 (ESV) tells us this is the very thing Jesus came to deliver us from!

> *"Since therefore the children share in flesh and blood, he himself likewise partook of the same things, that through death he might destroy the one who has the power of death, that is, the devil, **and deliver all those who through fear of death were subject to lifelong slavery."***

What would Jesus say to someone who is bound by fear? He would, of course, meet them with love. The Bible says:

> *"There is no fear in love; but perfect love casts out fear, because fear involves torment. But he who fears has not been made perfect in love."*
>
> 1 John 4:18

We need to come into alignment with how God sees us. We are not bound by fear. Death has no hold on us. When we align our hearts with how God sees us, the picture changes. He thinks only good thoughts toward us. He has only thoughts of peace. He has plans to prosper us and give us a wonderful future. Christ is so much greater than any tormenting spirit.

XII

Strength to Endure

As we boarded the medical flight to the children's hospital in Tennessee, I knew I had probably forgotten things I would need. In my hurry, I remember giving a house key to our pastors so they could go into our home and send us anything we needed. As it turned out, they took full advantage of that key!

When we returned home and walked through the front door, we felt *so* loved.

The refrigerator had been stocked with cheese, eggs, bacon, juice, bread, milk . . . someone had thoughtfully bought us food that we could 'grab and go'. Our laundry was folded. Our rent and electricity bills had been paid, so we didn't have to think about the tasks of life for a while.

Even today, I remember the love. The people in our church loved us *so well*. They gave us the strength to get through the early days when the grief was most intense.

Finding the strength to endure in difficult times is not always easy. Sometimes it takes everything we've got to say, "Today I'm going to get out of bed. I'm going to breathe in and out. I'm going to find something positive in my day." Other times, we need to draw on the love of others—those who feel our pain and want to help.

For me, having a job and going to work every day was a huge help. I didn't necessarily look forward to it. I would rather have stayed in bed or stayed at home. But I had to go to work. Thankfully, I was blessed with a supportive supervisor and a wonderful team who looked out for me. Work was not just a place to put my personal life on the back shelf for a while; it was a place for me to verbally process what had happened. My colleagues at work, whether they shared my faith or not, gave me the strength to keep moving forward.

I was also touched by the love and care of people I had never met. One friend was so deeply moved by my son's death that she wrote a poem, perfectly capturing who my son was. It blessed me so much that she cared enough to pour herself out on paper, and that she knew my son well enough to capture him in this poem. This friend was talking to her boss at work one day. He was a wealthy businessman in the area who had experienced his own tragedies in life. This man had never met our family, but when he heard what had happened, he was moved with compassion and wanted to help. He paid for our son's funeral expenses, the casket, the burial site, the headstone, everything. I hadn't even given any thought to the cost or how we could have paid for it all. But he paid for everything.

Pete and I were used to giving and helping others; now we were learning how to receive. In this season, there was no way for us to pay anyone back for what they gave. It was an overwhelming feeling to be loved and cared for so extravagantly. Our community blessed us in ways we could never have imagined. Like Jesus, they did for us what we could not do for ourselves, and it caused us to love them all the more.

Lifting the Burden

I shed many a tear thinking about the love that was shown to me and my family in those early days. The reality is, no one could make the pain disappear, but they could lift the daily burdens of things like getting groceries into my home, folding my laundry, paying my rent, and my electric bill. No one had the right words because there weren't words that would take care of the situation. But those simple little things spoke volumes about their love. The compassion of others caused me to feel so blessed at a time when I felt robbed and stolen from.

I realize this isn't the situation for everyone. Not everyone has colleagues or friends or a church family so caring and compassionate. But I do believe that one of the reasons that people rallied around us was because we had served so faithfully for so many years. It is true that in serving, you will be served yourself.

But being served requires a new level of vulnerability—especially for those who are in leadership. Some leaders believe they must be strong for everyone else and never show any weakness because they presume that would not be good leadership. The opposite is true. Going through difficult times and showing others you are vulnerable takes those relationships to another level. When people have seen us at our worst, the friendships run deep. The truth is, you can't stop the grief and the pain and the hurt, so you might as well be real about it. It shows people you're touchable, you're human. Yes, we're spiritual, and there's an element of spiritual maturity in each of us, but we all struggle and go through things just like anyone else.

We must not confuse what we are going through with who we are. If you are grieving, this is not who you fundamentally are—it's who you are right now, and for good reason! Think about Jesus in the Garden of Gethsemane, where He prayed regarding the cross and the death He was facing. Scripture says that He told his disciples that He began to be sorrowful and deeply distressed to the point that His sweat became like great drops of blood falling to the ground. He was facing death and in great distress. This is not who He fundamentally was, but in that moment, He struggled just like we do. Likewise, Peter, in a moment of weakness, denied Jesus three times. This doesn't change the fact that Peter was called by God to be a 'rock'. Yes, in that moment, he was weak. But fundamentally, that moment did not define Peter.

Jesus and Peter were not weak men. They were great leaders, but they had their moments of weakness. Moments of weakness just show that we are human, capable of mistakes, and grief, and sorrow.

This is why we must be moved by compassion. It is not easy for leaders to be vulnerable, but it opens opportunities for others to love on us. The truth is, we're more likely to reach out to one another when we're vulnerable. It's reciprocal. When others are going through something bad, we're ready to be there for them, just as they were for us. Needing others in our difficult seasons helps us identify with others when they are struggling. We remember back to when that was us, and we remember how it felt for us. This causes compassion to arise in our hearts, and so we reach out. What a powerful expression of the heart of God! Jesus said:

"By this all will know that you are my disciples, if you have love for one another."

John 13:35

Moved With Compassion

Throughout our journey, at the hospital, at the funeral, and in the weeks that followed, our friends and family would often comment about how strong I seemed to be. There is some truth to that. I remember ministering to people who had come to Keagan's funeral and praying for those who were grieving. One woman who had also lost a child came to the funeral only because she heard about what happened and wanted to be there. She was still grieving her son's loss and wanted to meet me. I remember just hugging her and praying that God would show Himself strong inside of her.

There was also an older couple from our church who Keagan had 'adopted' as grandparents. Seeing they were grieving so terribly, I grabbed them during the funeral and prayed for them as well. It wasn't that I didn't want people to pray for me—it was that I could see the grief others were feeling, and I wanted to help them, just as they wanted to help me. We all wanted to help each other get through.

◆ ◆ ◆

Recently, just before Pete and I got up to minister at a church in our city, the pastor shared with the congregation a little of our story and commented on how strong we were in the months following Keagan's death and how he remembered me praying for others during that time. I hear that a lot. I remember everyone kept telling me how strong I was and how they were so encouraged by the strength that my husband and I were showing.

I understand why. I'm sure on the outside it may have looked like strength, because we still showed up to church. I still led worship. I still prayed with my team before the service. But the truth is, I didn't feel strong; in fact, that's probably when I was at my weakest. I was still searching for what I had done wrong and where I had 'missed it'. I pulled away from God to an extent. I didn't pray for the longest time. Certainly, one-on-one prayer with God was not happening.

I wasn't being phony. I remember singing, "You have turned my mourning into dancing, and my sorrow into joy." I didn't feel that way—I was singing in the hope that one day that would be true. I sang because I knew God was still able to heal. I sang because I knew His Word was true. I didn't sing because I felt strong. I didn't sing because I was happy. I sang in faith. I sang because at my core, I believed it. I sang because I knew it would confuse the devil. I sang because I had to focus on what God had for me in the future. I sang at my weakest point, and God became strong inside of me.

Attributing Our Strength to God

At some point, it sank into my heart that the strength people were seeing was God's strength and not mine. It was God who carried me through that terrible time. I only looked strong because God was involved. I was a shell of a being, but I looked strong because God was the one standing up on the inside of me and strengthening me. It wasn't me at all.

2 Corinthians 12:7-10 talks about this very thing. It mentions that Paul had a 'thorn in his flesh'. Many people have said they believe that

Paul was dealing with a sickness or disease of some kind. I don't believe for one minute that the 'thorn in the flesh' Paul was talking about was a physical illness. The scripture plainly tells us it was "a messenger of Satan sent to buffet him." More than likely, Paul was referring to a difficult person or a straightforward spiritual attack. Maybe he was referring to his own thoughts tormenting him. Whatever it was, Paul describes it as "a messenger of Satan." Interestingly, after pleading with the Lord for him to take it away, God gives him this answer:

> *"My grace is sufficient for you . . . my strength is made perfect in weakness."*
>
> *1 Corinthians 12:9*

As a result, Paul responded:

> *"Therefore, I will all the more gladly boast in my weaknesses, so that the power of Christ may dwell in me. So, I am well pleased with weaknesses . . . for when I am weak [in human strength], then I am strong [truly able, truly powerful, truly drawing from God's strength]."*
>
> *1 Corinthians 12:10 AMP*

Paul is being vulnerable with his readers here. He's probably the most respected leader in the early church, yet he's real about his point of weakness. He knows that God is in the business of being strong when we are weak.

This is our testimony: *I am weak, but He is strong. I once was blind, but now I see. His strength is made perfect in my weakness. I was lost, but now I'm found. I was in darkness, and He brought me into His marvelous light.*

The truth is, our testimony is always about God's strength. It's never how we were so strong and able to conquer; it's always about how we are nothing and He is everything. So, if in your situation you feel helpless, just know that your Helper is near. It's okay to be weak. He gives power to the weak and strength to the powerless.

XIII

Encouraging Yourself in the Lord

One thing I've found over the course of my life is that encouragement ultimately has to come from ourselves—from our own soul, our own mind, our own voice.

It's not that God doesn't encourage us, or that people's encouragement doesn't matter. But basically, we live life in our own homes. Typically, we struggle when we're alone. It's at 2 a.m. when we're lying in bed or pacing the floor that our thoughts assail us.

> *This seems hopeless.*
> *It doesn't feel like it's ever going to get any better.*
> *I miss my loved one so much.*

I'm a 'fixer', so when I feel helpless, it's easy for me to go into 'do-ing mode' or to call a friend and say, "Hey, what should I do here?" Sure, there's a time and a place for that. But there comes a point in all our lives when we don't need to call a friend. We need to come to God as our source of encouragement and only *do* what He says.

For me, this usually looks like a good shouting church service. You know the sort, when it's just you and Jesus. You may start out feeling down, but before you know it, you've come to a joyful place, you've reached a high note where you can praise him anyway, knowing *this stinks, but I know who holds tomorrow. I know that He's got me.* There's a joy that comes with encouraging yourself in the Lord that's like nothing anyone else or any other environment can bring.

Countless times, I have found myself sad or discouraged or troubled by one thing or another. Each of us does well to know when we are most susceptible to this. For me, my sleep is very important. If I wake up in the night feeling anxious or downcast, I've trained myself to immediately switch my natural thinking to a spiritual standpoint. I'll say, "God, I need to rest. I'm going to lie down and close my eyes and then in the morning, when I'm well rested and my thoughts are clear, I'll bring this to you." Then I begin to pray in the Holy Spirit. This is an effective way to disengage from my thoughts and interrupt their flow. Before I know it, I'm drifting back off to sleep. In the morning when I wake, those thoughts might still be with me, but at least I don't have the stress of not having enough sleep.

I admit, even the next day, when I bring my difficulties to the Lord, it can feel like I'm trudging through mud. But as I begin to speak God's Word over my life and agree with what He says over my situation, the heaviness lifts. Right there, in my own home, on my own, I can tap into the true source of encouragement—His presence. Personally, I like to move. I often pace around the room, singing or declaring His promises, His character, His goodness. Soon enough, lightness comes, and the chaos lifts. I might even emerge with an action plan! But whatever the outcome, I come away with an assurance that God is with me, and He is helping me. I have encouraged *myself* in the Lord.

Along with loving others, being able to encourage yourself in the Lord is one of the greatest marks of maturity. Isaiah 61:3 speaks of "putting on the garment of praise for the spirit of heaviness." Why? So that we might be called "trees of righteousness, the planting of the Lord, that He may be glorified." There is a direct correlation in scripture between encouraging ourselves in the Lord and becoming planted, established, mature. No longer are we focused on ourselves or our problems. Our encouragement becomes a source of blessing *to others*.

Trees provide shade *for others*.

Trees provide shelter *for others*.

Trees provide food *for others*.

No tree starts out fully-grown, just as none of us start out as mature Christians. It's okay if you're not there yet. But you can make a start. Perhaps you can decide to go one day without reaching out to others for encouragement, and instead, seek your joy in the Lord. As strength comes and you get the hang of it, you might be able to go two days . . . or three. When it feels like you are being dragged down by endless nagging thoughts, start encouraging yourself with words like:

God is with me.

I'm never alone.

I'm never without help.

Soon you'll be thinking, *I can handle this!*

Strengthening Our Hearts

Like lifting weights or eating right, encouraging ourselves in the Lord is a discipline. It takes time, but it soon becomes second nature. The more you do it, the more it becomes your default position. Those who are prone to discouragement may need to work hard to exercise this muscle. But don't be fooled—this isn't something for some personality types and not others. If you have any ability at all to encourage yourself, you need to flex that muscle. Once you can lift yourself up, you'll be in a position to lift others—and to teach them to do it for themselves!

There were times in walking through my son's death that I had no choice but to encourage myself in the Lord. If I didn't put a halt to wrong thinking and jump-start some right thinking, I could easily have ended up in the pit of despair. Being in the pit of despair doesn't mean that God is not there with you—He is—but like David the psalmist, it does mean you will have to dig deep into your resolve and find whatever trace of fight you still possess:

> *"I waited patiently for the Lord, and He inclined to me and heard my cry. He also brought me up out of a horrible pit, out of the miry clay, and set my feet upon a rock, and established my steps. He has put a new song in my mouth—praise to our God; many will see it and fear, and will trust in the Lord."*
>
> *Psalm 40:1-3*

What situation was David facing? He and his men had returned from battle to find that their enemies had burned their village and homes. The women and children had been taken captive and carried away. When David and his men saw this, they lifted their voices and wept until they had no more power to weep. Can you imagine? These men had just returned from battle. They'd left it all on the field. They were exhausted to the point where two hundred of the men who had fought with David were so weary they could not even cross the brook to get home (1 Samuel 30:9-10).

Not only were David and his men worn out physically, they were hit emotionally. What do people naturally do when faced with tragedy? They look for someone to blame. In their case, it was their leader. *This was on David.* Before long, David's men were talking about stoning him to death.

Imagine David's distress. Not only were his wives and children gone, but the wives and children of all his men were gone—and he felt the responsibility of that. With the very men he had just fought alongside now against him, and no one to encourage him, we could understand if David had curled up in a ball and cried as his men stoned him to death.

But that isn't what he did. The scriptures tell us that he "encouraged himself in the Lord." I wish we knew how he did that.

> *Did he cry out to God?*
> *Did he remind himself of how God had always come through before?*
> *Did he rehearse times when he heard the voice of God and acted on it, and God delivered him?*
> *Did he declare that God would never leave him or forsake him?*
> *Did he remember a song from his days as a shepherd?*

Whatever he did, he took the time to strengthen himself in the Lord his God. Only then, when his heart was encouraged, did he ask God for an action plan. *Should he pursue his enemy?* God answered him immediately with a strategy and a promise. Yes, he should pursue his enemy, overtake them, and recover *everything*.

That is exactly what happened.

> *"So David recovered all that the Amalekites had carried away, and David rescued his two wives. And nothing of theirs was lacking, either small or great, sons or daughters, spoil or anything which they had taken from them; David recovered all."*
>
> *1 Samuel 30:18-19*

Summoning Our Soul

When things get bad, we must be able to encourage ourselves in the Lord. David did this often. In Psalm 42, he remembers better days. He goes back and forth for a while, as if he's trudging through mud, trying to summon his soul out of despair:

> *"Why are you cast down, O my soul? And why are you disquieted within me? Hope in God, for I shall yet praise Him." (v. 5)*

Eventually, he breaks out of his discouragement.

> *"The Lord will command His lovingkindness in the daytime, and in the night His song shall be with me—a prayer to the God of my life." (v. 8)*

There is amazing power in being able to lift ourselves out of the doldrums. In Psalm 103:1-5, David instructs his soul and mind to bless the Lord. It's as if he's not giving himself a choice. He is *telling* himself to forget not all God's benefits—and then he lists them out:

> *He forgives your iniquities*
> *He heals your diseases.*
> *He redeems your life from destruction.*
> *He crowns you with lovingkindness and tender mercies.*
> *He satisfies your mouth with good things so that your*
> *youth is renewed like the eagle's.*

This is how you encourage yourself in the Lord. You start declaring the truths you know. You remember God. You remember His goodness. You remember how He has redeemed you. You remember the benefits of your ever-loving savior. You speak what you know to be true over what you are feeling.

> *"I may feel overcome with grief, but I know God is my help."*
> *"Weeping may endure for a night, but joy comes in the*
> *morning."*
> *"The One who lives in me is greater than my enemies."*

As well as declaring these truths, we can sing of the goodness of God. A song of joy or praise is good medicine and will always encourage your heart! The apostle Paul writes:

> *"Be filled with the Spirit . . . speaking to one another in*
> *psalms and hymns and spiritual songs, singing and making*
> *melody in your heart to the Lord, giving thanks always*

for all things to God the Father in the name of our Lord Jesus Christ."

Ephesians 5:18-20

One night, my husband Pete was out with some guys from the church. They'd had a great time together, and Pete's spirits were lifted. But as he dropped his friend off and turned towards home with only himself in the car, his thoughts suddenly accosted him. *You stood in faith, but your son died anyway.*

Thankfully, Pete recognized this as a spiritual attack. Speaking aloud, he said, "Devil, you may throw whatever you like at me, but I will outlast you! Whatever obstacles you put in my path, whatever thoughts of discouragement, whatever doubt or fear you throw at me, I won't quit. I will outlast this barrage of thoughts and discouragement."

That declaration was like a shot in the arm of faith and boldness. From that moment on, Pete's heart was strengthened. He knew his faith would endure, no matter what Satan threw at him. He had learned to fend off discouragement in the presence of the Lord.

Stirring Our Expectation

Encouraging ourselves in the Lord stirs up expectation. We don't know *what* God is going to do. We don't know *when* He's going to do it, but we know He's up to something, and it's always going to be good!

I recall a time when I had encouraged myself so much in the Lord that I just expected God's goodness! There was nothing tangible I could connect to it—I just knew that I would be a recipient of His goodness, and that it would come at any time ... and all the time! My heart was in a constant state of expectation. Whatever the need, I just expected God to intervene and bring help. I expected something miraculous—to the point where I was excited about even the day-to-day activities.

> *I was excited to walk up the road to get the mail.*
> *I was excited to go to church.*
> *I was excited to see what the next day would hold.*

The years of dealing with the fear of death were gone. Now I found myself singing: "I will not die but live to tell what He has done" (Psalm 118:17). When I wasn't singing a song that had already been written, I would sing a song from my heart. Many times, it wasn't in tune or perfect, but that didn't matter. I was declaring out loud with my mouth the promises of God. I was encouraging my own heart in the Lord.

I often think of Viktor Frankl, a man who survived four different concentration camps. In one of those camps, he was given the task of hauling dead bodies to the burn pits to be disposed of. I can't think of a more horrible existence. Day after day, he was faced with bringing the corpses of people he knew and loved to those pits. Yet in his book, *Man's Search for Ultimate Meaning,* he wrote these words:

> *"Everything can be taken from a man but one thing:*
> *the last of human freedoms—to choose one's attitude in*
> *any given set of circumstances, to choose one's own way."*

Viktor Frankl survived the holocaust by choosing daily to look for the good. He would imagine his wife encouraging him. He would look for humor in situations, even if only for a brief moment. He did what it took to bring hope and encouragement to his soul.

We may not be dealing with the same level of despair and depravity as Viktor Frankl, but like him, we must hone our ability to encourage ourselves. We will all get to a point in life when external encouragement is not adequate for the burdens we bear. In those times, this is the mark of maturity: that we strengthen *ourselves* in the Lord.

XIV

Relaxing Into the Love of God

When we are in the midst of one of life's storms, relaxing is the last thing on our minds. We become stressed out; our thoughts are consumed with the issue at hand. There's no way to ignore what is going on, of course, but while we stress over life's problems, it's important to remember that Jesus is with us, and He is not stressed.

Remember the disciples in the storm? A lot of them were fishermen— they were used to sudden changes in weather patterns. I'm sure they'd navigated rough seas before. But this was different. The waves were threatening to sink the boat. No wonder they were stressed. No wonder they were anxious. From what they knew of their experience, this was a storm they might not make it through.

> *"And when he got into the boat, his disciples followed him. And behold, there arose a great storm on the sea, so that the boat was being swamped by the waves; but he*

was asleep. And they went and woke him, saying, 'Save us, Lord; we are perishing.' And he said to them, 'Why are you afraid, O you of little faith?' Then he rose and rebuked the winds and the sea, and there was a great calm. And the men marveled, saying, 'What sort of man is this, that even winds and sea obey him?'"

Matthew 8:23-27 ESV

I find this amusing. It wasn't like Jesus wasn't perishing too. He was in the boat with them. If they were going down, He was going down too! And yet, He was asleep. Wasn't the water hitting Him? Was He so tired that it didn't even phase Him?

But the disciples saw it as a lack of care. "Don't you *care* that we're going to die?!"

Jesus did care, of course, just as He cares for us. But it wasn't the storm or the thought of sinking that fazed Jesus. It was the lack of faith His disciples showed in that moment on the sea. "Why are you so fearful?" He asked. "Why is it that you have *no faith?*"

Every time we face a tumultuous situation, we have a choice: Will we respond with fear? Or will we respond with faith in who Jesus is? In the moment, it's easy to panic, to see the worst possible outcome, to let our minds wander down those dark alleys where we begin to prepare for the worst-case scenario.

The truth is, we can't see around those corners. But God can. When we fundamentally trust He has our very best interests on His heart, we can rest—even in the midst of life's storms.

I do concede, however, that the language we often read in the Bible doesn't remind us of relaxing. Sure, the Bible says, "Do not be anxious," but more frequently, we read words like,

> *"Fight the good fight . . ." (2 Timothy 4:7)*
> *"Seek peace and pursue it . . ." (Psalm 34:14)*
> *"Endeavor to keep the unity of the Spirit . . ." (Ephesians 4:3)*
> *"Lay hold of eternal life . . ." (1 Timothy 6:12)*
> *"Press toward the mark . . ." (Philippians 3:14)*

These are all very active verbs. It's almost 'striving towards excellence' kind of language. It doesn't give a picture of relaxing.

So what is our position? Are we to contend, or are we to rest? I have found that resting in the love of God is the deepest expression of faith during trials. We're not talking about living on autopilot, or adopting an attitude of *que sera sera*, or falling asleep at the wheel. We may still need to bail some water out of the boat and do whatever it takes to stay on course—but we do so from a place of peace. A place of trust. A place of relaxation into the love of God. Knowing that whatever comes our way, He will help us navigate a path through it.

Relaxed in His Love

Staying steady in the storms of life can take substantial effort. Everything around us is in turmoil. There's uncertainty on every side. Sometimes it takes all our strength just to stay on our feet. But what about our heart posture? Is our heart tossed about, or is it steady even in the storm? If our heart posture is *toward God,* we can relax and allow Him to handle the unknowns. If our heart is toward Him, how much more is His heart toward those who trust Him and rely on Him? Does that mean we won't have difficulties? Absolutely not! It does however, mean that He will direct us through those difficult times.

> *"In all your ways acknowledge Him, and He will direct your paths."*
>
> Proverbs 3:6

If my path leads me into a tragedy, He's going to lead me through it. If He leads me into the boat, He's going to get me through the storm.

When we talk about relaxing in the love of God, it doesn't negate the active component of our faith. But when all that we do is from a foundation of trust and rest in His lovingkindness towards us, that's faith. We rest in God, knowing that His ways are good for us. We relax into the love of God, trusting that He will guide us. Sometimes He will prompt us to 'fight the good fight' or show us some other active response. But as believers, everything we do, we do from a place of relaxing in His love.

This is how we follow the leading and guiding of the Holy Spirit. In fact, being *led* by the Holy Spirit is really what relaxing in His love is all about.

> *"However, when He, the Spirit of truth, has come, He will guide you into all truth; for He will not speak on His own authority, but whatever He hears He will speak; and He will tell you things to come."*
>
> John 16:13

Notice that John 16:13 says, "He will tell us things to come." He knows what lies ahead. In the natural, it's okay to do what we can. But ultimately, if we are to stay in peace as we navigate difficulty, we need to surrender to the leading of the Holy Spirit. As Kenneth Hagin often said, "The answer to a million questions is: *Be led by the Spirit of God.*"

Knowing the character of God is helpful to us. Reading the Bible is important too. But there's an *intangible* element called 'the leading of the Holy Spirit' which absolutely vital. It is the Spirit who gives us life. We cannot live without the leading of the Spirit. Sometimes it's a thought that comes to you—perhaps you feel that you're supposed to do something, so you go and do that thing. Resting in God comes when we simply obey those promptings, and leave everything else up to God.

When we operate from this default place of relaxing in the love of God, we find ourselves more able to discern when He is trying to lead us out of a harmful situation or help us to avoid trouble in our lives. We must not allow our spirit to become cluttered by panic and worry. The antidote to inner turmoil is trusting in the love of God and staying perceptive to the leading of His Spirit.

The truth is, there are so many circumstances we can't control, so many things we need to surrender—not in the sense of 'giving up' but of handing over the details of our lives and hearts to the One who loves us passionately and unceasingly.

Mercy All Around Us

When our heart's posture is toward God, we begin to see that there is mercy all around us. We are not subject to all that life throws at us. We are sustained and delivered by His mercy. I love that many of David's psalms simply say, "Have mercy on me, O Lord, have mercy" (e.g. Psalm 6:2-4).

Mercy doesn't minimize what we are going through. I recently prayed for an eight-year-old boy in our church who is suffering from a rare bone disorder. The little guy is wracked with pain. There is no known cure. How else do you pray? "Lord, have mercy."

A neighbor of mine was recently diagnosed with colon cancer. The doctors removed her colon, and she looks good right now, but there's not a good prognosis. I told her, "The Bible says, if we lay hands on the sick, they shall recover."

"Put your hands on me!" she said.

I held her hands and prayed with her for healing. Then I finished with, "God, have mercy on her like you did with the woman with the issue of blood."

So often we think being 'cast on the mercy of God' is what happens when we are at the end of all our options. But God's mercy is a renewable resource. His mercies are new every morning. Lamentations 3:22-23 (ESV) says,

> "The steadfast love of the Lord never ceases; his mercies
> never come to an end; they are new every morning; great
> is your faithfulness."

Notice that verse is in the present tense, not future tense. His mercy is a daily thing that we can draw upon. Since mercy is for today, let's not get ahead of God. Tomorrow is in His hands.

We tend to get anxious about situational things in our lives—who we're going to marry, where we're going to buy a house, whether we should take this job or that one, what our calling is . . . Remember, in all of this, God has our best interests at heart. He'll make the details evident. We don't need to fret or be consumed with thoughts of working it all out. As we come to a place of peace and rest, our emotional turmoil is stilled. We adopt a heart posture that says, *I'm listening to you God. I want to do your will. I'm trusting you to lead and guide me.* When we rest in His love, we don't need to worry that we're going to miss God's leading.

Fixing Our Eyes on Jesus

It's common for us to worry about stuff, but worry is like an indicator light on the dashboard of your car. It's just a warning, a sign that something needs attention. When the indicator light of worry comes on, it's telling us it's time to pray. Fretting about things outside of prayer is worry. That's why 1 Peter 5:7 exhorts us to cast all our cares on Him, because He cares for us. Remember the disciples' question to Jesus in the storm, "Don't you care . . .?"

His answer is always *yes.*

I recall a race car driver once saying, "You go where you look." When they're taking a tight corner, they're not looking down at the road; they're focusing on the exit point, they're looking to where they are going. That's how they steer the car out of a tight spot and finish the race. The same is true in life.

What are your eyes focused on? Are you looking at the dilemma, or are you looking to Jesus? It's easy to become fixated on the worst-case scenario, especially in the face of challenges. But let's remember that God is with us. He knows the path and outcome. When our eyes are on Jesus, we do not question His care for us. He desires that we should have life *more abundantly.* Let's shift our heart posture. With eyes on Jesus, we can fully relax in His love.

God Looks Ahead

Most of us are familiar with the name of God, Jehovah Jirah. It means 'the God who provides'. But did you know there's more to it than that? The full meaning of the name is, 'The God who *looks ahead* and makes provision'. In other words, He doesn't just provide for the needs of the day. He's already looked around the corners of your life, and He's already made a way. He's already got the answer. He's already supplied your need.

Think of how God looked ahead through time and made a way for us by sending Jesus. That was thought out and planned from the beginning. Think about Abraham taking Isaac to sacrifice him (Genesis 22:3-16). God had already prepared a ram in the thicket. He'd already looked ahead and made provision. Genesis 22:14 tells us:

"Abraham called that place, 'The Lord will provide.'"

Paul and Silas knew this truth about God too. They'd been beaten, then placed in the 'inner prison' where they were chained, possibly facing execution. Yet their response was to sing and pray. I don't think they were singing, "Break every chain." I think they were magnifying the Lord. They were resting in His love for them.

"About midnight Paul and Silas were praying and singing hymns to God, and the prisoners were listening to them."
Acts 16:25

How do we know these two men weren't panicking? Because when the prison doors flew open, Paul and Silas didn't flee. They didn't rush out thanking God for their miracle. They were able to minister peace to the godless prison guard (who *was* panicking. He was ready to throw himself on his sword!).

Look at what happened next:

> "*The guard took Paul and Silas to his house. He washed their stripes. He brought them into his home and set food and drink before them. And then they glorified God together.*"
> *Acts 16:34 (author's paraphrase)*

What an outcome! When we simply relax in the love of God, we become not just recipients, but transmitters, of peace!

XV

The Overflow of Compassion

"If you're going through hell, keep going."
—*Winston Churchill*

As humans, we will all experience trauma in one form or another. Perhaps it's the death of someone we love. Or a catastrophic accident. Or sickness. Bankruptcy. A volatile home or work environment . . .

Our hearts can be broken and beaten down in many ways.

When we are dealing with trauma, it becomes difficult to see beyond our situation. Invariably, we turn inwards, we become self-centered. And that's okay—at least, for a while. It's important to focus on self-care, to treat ourselves gently, and to lean on others for help, especially godly counselors.

But if we're not careful, self-centeredness can become habitual. The trauma we once lived through can quickly become our identity. This happens when we remain fixated on the trauma *beyond its time.* Have you ever met someone who has become stuck in a cycle or a season of grief? They've turned inwards . . . and stayed inwards. These people often end up becoming takers instead of givers.

Grief has a season. It has a natural endpoint. When it is prolonged, it becomes *unnatural.* This is why we must learn to recognize when our season of grief is over. This isn't easy. When we experience trauma, we can end up feeling so neglected, so hurt (or, like me, so 'spiritually raped') that we feel like it *should* be all about us. But at some point, we need to stop and ask ourselves, "How can I turn this tragedy into something that God can use for good, instead of something horrible that happened to me?" When we make that shift, it's likely we'll find it a nice little break to think of someone else rather than ourselves.

Making Someone Else's Day

I was at work one day, thinking about what a hard time I'd been having with some relationships. Things weren't going my way, and at my desk that morning, I found myself shedding some tears. All I wanted to do was to seclude myself. *I just want to shut my office door and not interact with anyone,* I decided.

Then I thought about my co-workers, and the narrative changed. *I have to pull myself together,* I told myself. *This is not a good place to set up camp.* Right then, I made a difficult but brave decision: *My day may be ruined, but I wasn't going to allow someone else's day to be ruined.*

Then I came up with a way to shift the focus from me to them. Pulling myself together, I made a list of the twenty-two people I shared an office with, opened my Sonic App, and placed an order for everyone's favorite drink. Then I walked out of the office, ran down the road, and picked them all up. You can imagine how fun it was to deliver those drinks! As I handed each of my staff their favorite drink, I told them how much I appreciated their hard work. Then I asked if there was anything I could do for them that day. *Was there a job they were dreading, like cleaning the bathrooms or dealing with a client who was difficult?* I told them I would do it if they wanted me to. To my delight, some took me up on it! Others just appreciated the offer. But more importantly, the moment I focused on blessing others rather than feeling miserable about my situation, the mood in the whole building lightened! Soon, everyone was laughing. I knew there was no way of making *my* day better, but I sure could make someone else's day better!

◆ ◆ ◆

Seeing and acknowledging those around us is key to moving forward. And it takes intentionality. I remember the day I stood at the cemetery looking at Keagan's headstone. As I lifted my head and began looking around, my eyes fell on another tombstone, and then another. One had the names of two brothers on it. *That momma lost two kiddos, not just one,* I thought. Then I saw a tombstone that had the birth and the death date on it—just one day apart. *I'd had four years with Keagan. That momma only got one day.* I thought about parents who had lost their children to suicide. Keagan was so full of life. He laughed every day. *Imagine grieving the loss of a child, knowing they didn't love life and didn't feel there was any other solution.*

The reality is, so many others have experienced the loss of a child. So many others have faced the same trauma we have. It's a sobering thought. I look at people differently now. I feel a lot more compassion— not just for the ones who are going through dark times. I feel for the people who have become stuck in the loop of sadness or grief or trauma.

The Power of Compassion

It can be confronting to look beyond ourselves. Our natural tendency is to judge, or to look away. The challenge is to see others, not with natural eyes, but through the eyes of Jesus.

Jesus was *filled* with compassion.

He saw the needs of others and was moved in his heart . . . to action. In Luke 7:12-15 we read:

> *"And when He came near the gate of the city, behold, a dead man was being carried out, the only son of his mother; and she was a widow. And a large crowd from the city was with her. When the Lord saw her, **He had compassion on her** and said to her, 'Do not weep'. Then he came and touched the open coffin, and those who carried him stood still. And He said, 'Young man, I say to you, arise'. So he who was dead sat up and began to speak. And He presented him to his mother."*

For Jesus, action always flowed from compassion.

He weeps at the tomb of Lazarus . . . then He calls him forth.

He sees the hungry multitude . . . then He feeds them.

He notices the woman caught in adultery . . . then He saves her life.

At the moment of His greatest betrayal, Jesus sees His disciple cut off a man's ear . . . and He reaches out to heal him.

He looks to the man on the cross beside Him . . . and promises him paradise.

Redefining the Gospel

Can you imagine what miracles could happen if each of us were to look beyond ourselves and allow the compassion of Jesus to touch our hearts? This is how we are called to live! This is the Great Commission! As believers, we go into the world and we preach the gospel. We are the bearers of good news!

To someone who is sick, we say: *Jesus is the healer!*

To someone who is poor, we declare: *Jesus is the provider!*

To someone who is lonely, or in despair, we remind them: *Jesus is near. He is the friend who sticks closer than a brother. He offers hope and a future.*

But what makes the good news real to those we meet? It's us. *We* are His hands and feet. What makes compassion so powerful is that it is fundamentally *practical.*

Whenever Jesus *felt* something, He *did* something.

The Good Samaritan exemplified this. He saw a man in need, and he crossed the street. He cleaned the man's wounds, he bound them up. He put him on his own donkey and took him to an inn. He paid the innkeeper to care for him and feed him. Those are all very simple, practical things, but to the injured man . . . they were life!

A Room for a Night

Lifting one another up is something any of us can do. We don't need a college degree to act compassionately towards others. We simply need to offer our time, our money, our effort, a listening ear, an encouraging word, a meal or a ride . . . or maybe even a room for the night.

I'll never forget what our pastor did for Pete and I when we returned to Missouri after Keagan's death. "Come and stay the night at our house," he said. "Don't go to your home. At some point, you're going to need to face it, but for tonight, come to our house." The truth is, nothing in either of us wanted to go back to our own home. We were so numb and so sad we just got in the car with our pastors and let them take us to their house.

That evening when it came time to get ready for bed, Pastor Guy turned to us. "You guys go get ready and get into bed," he said. "I'm going to come down and sit with you awhile." A few minutes later, Guy came into our room, sat beside our bed, and while we drifted off to sleep, he gently read scripture over us.

What an act of love.

That night, pastor Guy wasn't trying to offer us a sermon. He was simply being a good shepherd. He wanted us to be at peace. He didn't want us to be alone in the dark with our thoughts running wild. What a comfort it was to fall asleep that night with the sacred, familiar words of scripture being spoken over us by a fatherly, loving voice. I'm sure some might think his actions intrusive—coming into our bedroom, sitting beside our bed. But pastor Guy understood that in that moment of our lives, we simply needed care and compassion.

Lightening the Load

So here we are, twenty-three years later. Back then, I could never have imagined my son's life still breathing life into other people, but it is.

I couldn't have imagined being this happy back then.

But I am.

Life is so good. My kids are thriving. I don't feel stressed or anxious. I have a great group of friends and a wonderful church. The stench of death doesn't hang on me. People who haven't heard our story wouldn't know the grief we've journeyed through.

How I wish this could be true for each of us.

My neighbor shared with me one day that her life as a child was pure hell because her parents lost a child and never recovered. She ended up having to live with her grandparents because they couldn't move past the grief. "I know God has helped you," she said, "because you and Pete are so full of life. I never would have guessed that you had experienced anything like what my parents did."

This is the power of our story. It doesn't stop with the grief and trauma. I'm on the other side of it now, but others are in the middle of theirs. If I can encourage them to pick themselves up, dust themselves off, stand up on the track and keep running, then my story has come full circle.

Who is there who could benefit from your story?

There is more to life than just getting through your particular difficulty or tragedy. Every one of us goes through battles. Will we turn inward too long? If we can start looking toward others, our own troubles will begin to fall away. But we need to be intentional about this. The Bible says we must *lay aside* every weight and the sin that easily entangles us (Hebrews 12:1). If you have been carrying a weight of grief, I urge you today to lay it aside. Jesus' heart is for the weary and heavy-laden. He is not judging you. He is not unkind. But when we lift our gaze away from ourselves and look to Jesus, we begin to see the world through His eyes.

Who do you know who is carrying a heavy load? When we lay down our own load, we have more capacity for others. Don't worry, there will be others who will come along and pick up your load too! This race we call life isn't about who wins—it's about crossing the finish line together.

Think of the people who have lightened your load. I have a friend who used to show up at Walmart with a cardboard sign that read: I have a job, I have food, how can I help you? She would listen to people's request, then go into Walmart with them and purchase what they needed. One lady was buying a microwave for her daughter; someone else needed gas to get home; someone else was dealing with a sickness. Yes, my friend prayed for these people—but then she met their physical need. She allowed her heart to be *moved* with compassion. Yet what most people didn't see is that my friend's life was far from easy. She had her own burdens to carry, her own set of concerns. But this time, for just a while, she chose to set aside the weight and lighten the load of others.

All Creation Groans

It's not only individuals and families who need their load lightened. It's entire communities, people groups, nations . . .

Romans 8:22 tells us that "all of creation groans" in one way or another. The reality is, some topics are too big for us to address as one person. Homelessness, hunger, poverty, the fallout of war, natural disasters, trafficking, abuse . . . childhood cancer.

These are loads that need to be lifted on a greater scale.

When my son Reece was about ten years old, I began talking to him about how he had everything he needed on the inside of him to change the world. As he left home for school each day, I'd ask, "How do you change the world, Reece?" He'd think about it, and I would prompt him: *One day at a time, one person at a time.* Each afternoon when he arrived home from school, I'd ask, "Did you change the world today?" At first, Reece just smiled and said no. So I helped him out.

"Did you make someone laugh?

Did you do something kind?

Did you help someone?"

Before long, Reece was looking for opportunities to change the world, one day at a time, one person at a time.

"Someone dropped their books in the hallway, and I stopped to help pick them up."

"Someone was having a bad day, and I encouraged them."

"Someone didn't have a pencil, and I gave them mine."

Even at the age of ten, my son understood that small acts of kindness can lighten the load of someone who is struggling. Now that Reece is a young adult, he's thinking about how he can reach more people. He wants to do something he loves—but for a greater purpose. He wants to change the world!

Ministering to Multitudes

Jesus saw the individuals who sat on the roadside crying out, "Jesus, have mercy on me." He responded in compassion toward each one. But He also saw the multitude who had been with Him three days and were fainting with hunger. Jesus' response to the multitude was the same as His response to the individuals He ministered to day by day: *He was filled with compassion.*

In Matthew 15:32 we read:

*"Now Jesus called his disciples to Himself and said, 'I **have compassion on the multitude,** because they have now continued with Me three days and have nothing to eat. And I do not want to send them away hungry lest they faint on the way.'"*

I'm sure when the disciples heard Jesus say these words, their minds began searching for solutions. In the natural, their options were limited. *Did Jesus have a plan?* Maybe, but Jesus was lifting their expectations. He wanted them to realize not only what *He* could do, but what *they* could do.

The truth is, it rarely requires a miracle for us to help an individual. But when the multitudes are needy, it's a different story. For most of us, it's beyond our capacity to relieve suffering on a large scale. And yet that is exactly what Jesus asked His disciples to do.

How do we lighten the load of the world around us? By partnering with Jesus! The Bible teaches that we will do all that Jesus did . . . and greater! (John 14:12).

As the disciples worked alongside Jesus that day, four thousand people were fed! None of the disciples alone could have met the need of so many, but when they saw the compassion of Jesus and participated with Him, something incredible happened. Jesus took what little they had—just seven loaves and a few small fish—and He multiplied it!

So many people read stories like this and say, "I would have loved to have been there!" All we have to do is lift up our eyes. We are there! This is for today, for you and me! People all over the world are suffering. Do we share His compassion?

Look at Matthew chapter nine. Jesus is going through all the cities and villages, teaching, preaching the gospel, and healing those who are sick. That's the ones and twos. But in verses 36-38 we read,

> *"When He saw **the multitudes,** He was moved with compassion for them, because they were weary and scattered, like sheep having no shepherd. Then He said to His disciples, 'The harvest truly is plentiful, but the laborers are few. Therefore, pray the Lord of the harvest to send out laborers into His harvest.'"*

Interestingly, the very next thing Jesus does is to call His disciples together and give them authority to cast out unclean spirits and to heal *all kinds of sickness* and *all kinds of disease.* Why did He give them His authority? So that they too could minister freedom and healing in Jesus' name.

If only we would take our places as children of the Most High God and just get out there and be led with compassion. I have no doubt that God would show up in such a miraculous way that the government would no longer have to help with food, the world's greatest crises would be solved, our hospitals would have plenty of empty beds, and doctors would be confounded.

How do we partner with God for something that is beyond ourselves? We do our part. We tap into God and ask, "What's on your heart today?" We allow ourselves to be moved with compassion. For me, I just keep putting my hands on people, praying for people. It's up to God to show up. But my heart has been enlarged. I see sickness and disease, especially in the body of Christ, and all I can think is, "This isn't how it should be."

Have I got a formula? No. I don't think there is one.

Have I healed multitudes? No, but I'm open to it.

All I know is that I continue to believe for miracles.

I know there's more.

Today, I'm not contending for the life of one little boy. I'm speaking life over those who are on the path with me. But I'm also praying big prayers.

I want a cure for cancer.

I'd love to kick the devil in the teeth with that. He's taken one child out, but my son's death has caused me to rise up, and I'm not willing to back off. It seems everybody I know, knows someone who has been affected by cancer. It's the scourge of our generation. But there's an answer to cancer, and I know that answer lies with God. I'm praying God's will into this earth. And I believe that if we all join together, God will speak to someone about a cure for cancer, just like He spoke to someone about how to develop penicillin.

The suffering of the multitude is too great for God to ignore.

But we have to stay on it. We cannot afford to step aside and let cancer run amok. We have to keep asking, keep praying, and we must keep our hearts tender. We must remain motivated by compassion. We're going to get there!

What stirs your heart the most? Perhaps it's trafficking. Or child brides. Or refugees. Or abused women. Or crime. Or pornography. Or illiteracy. Or the plight of orphans. Some of us are passionate about strengthening marriages and families. Or financial management. Or economic reform. Or disaster recovery. Or building homes. Or digging wells. Or veteran care. Or mental health. Or suicide prevention. Or teens in crisis. Or helping people find their purpose. Or planting churches.

We're all given different gifts and abilities. Why? So that each one of us can partner with God for the thing that moves His heart. Because no matter how dark or difficult things are, *this changes nothing*. God is still powerful. God is still moved with compassion. God is still looking for people to be His hands and feet. And miracles still happen. He is the same yesterday, today and forever.

Through Him, we *can* change the world!

This Changes Nothing
- STUDY GUIDE -

1. DEATH IS NOT AN OPTION

1. *"God was our healer. My son wasn't going to die. I was standing in agreement with God's Word, believing, and most of all, speaking it out."* Keagan's diagnosis brought Jessica to a crossroads where she chose faith over fear. What is your perspective on 'choosing' faith? When have you chosen faith over fear? How did that impact you and your circumstances?

2. *"As humans, when we hear the worst, we naturally want to grasp for something. For Pete and me, it was prayer."* What do you know about God that helps you to trust Him when you are facing circumstances outside of your control?

3. Why was it important to Jessica that her words aligned with the power and goodness of God? In 2 Corinthians 4:13, Paul said, "I believed, and therefore I spoke." Which of God's promises do you most need to believe and speak over your life today?

4. Read Proverbs 18:21. Are there any words or statements you need to refrain from using? Write down or share three faith and hope-filled statements that you could use instead.

5. A strong church community wrapped love and compassion around Pete and Jessica. Who could you lean on in difficult times? What can you do this week to strengthen your support network?

6. David and Goliath's story helped Keagan understand the nature of the battle he was fighting. *"I wish I had a slingshot to throw rocks at the sickness!"* Keagan said. *"Your words are like rocks,"* I encouraged him. *"Throw 'em!"* Which biblical character or story is most meaningful to you—and why?

EXTRA STUDY: Read Numbers 13 and 14. Of the twelve men sent to spy on the Promised Land, note the difference in attitude between

those who chose faith and those who chose fear. What effect did the spies'
unbelief have on the Israelite community? What did God say about the
two who chose faith?

2. DESPERATE PRAYERS

1. *"Pete and I were full of faith. Our child was going to be healed, along with every child on that ward!"* Amid their own crisis, Pete and Jessica prayed for healing for other children and helped parents in small, practical ways. Why do you think faith is so strongly linked to compassion? What does it look like to have one without the other?

2. Unable to shield Keagan from the pain of medical interventions, Jessica felt guilt, shame, powerlessness, and like *"the most horrible mom in the world."* What hope do the following promises offer when we're feeling powerless: Psalm 30:5; Isaiah 43:2; John 14:2; 2 Corinthians 12:9?

3. Keagan's last words, "Magic Kingdom," hint that God had given him a glimpse of heaven. Picture the fulfillment of Revelation 21:4. How do these promises anchor your heart in peace?

4. In these scriptures, what was each person's response to the threat of death?
    a. 1 Samuel 17:22-26 (David hearing Goliath's taunts)
    b. 1 Kings 18:1-19:3 (Elijah being threatened by Jezebel)
    c. Matthew 8:5-13 (A centurion's servant facing a deathly illness)

5. There are many ways we can respond to difficult news. Underline any phrases that stand out to you in these passages:
    a. Proverbs 3:5-6   b. Psalm 37:1-5
    c. Psalm 62:8   d. Psalm 56:3

e.   Matthew 17:20

6.   In what area are you tempted to lean on your own understanding? Think of a specific situation where it is hard for you to trust God. Take a moment to declare the scriptures you have just read over these situations.

EXTRA STUDY: Skim through the gospels, taking note of all the occasions when Jesus encountered sickness, and His response in each situation. What does this tell us about God's ability and desire for people to be healed?

3. TOE-TO-TOE WITH THE DEVIL

1.   Physically, Jessica fell apart and sobbed. Spiritually, she felt vicious and bear-like, fighting for her son's life, toe-to-toe with the devil. Read the following scriptures:

   a.   Ephesians 6:18   b.   Romans 8:26-27
   c.   1 Corinthians 14:14-15

   How has the Spirit helped you when you didn't know how to pray? Share an experience where you received a breakthrough by engaging with God through prayer in the Spirit.

2.   *"I'd given it everything I could. It was all prayed out. There was nothing left but to thank God that He had heard me and answered my cry."* How does thanking God reflect faith in Him, even though our prayers are yet to be answered? Why does thanking Him result in the believer experiencing God's peace?

3.   What would breakthrough look like in your situation? Take a moment to thank God for the outcome, even before you see it.

4.   Scripture encourages us to go to God for wisdom. What questions do you have about a personal challenge you're facing? Take a moment to ask God your questions, then sit quietly for a few

moments. Write down or share any words, pictures, or 'impressions' that come to you during this time.

5. In what way does not having all the answers impact your relationship with God? What encouragement do you find in 1 Corinthians 13:9-12?

6. Read Hebrews 11, underlining any words that stand out about the nature of faith. (e.g., persevered, believed). What aspect of faith is God highlighting to you today?

EXTRA STUDY: To help you put the framework of God's character around your situation, find a Bible study on the names of God (e.g., Jehovah-Rohi: The Lord My Shepherd; Jehovah Jirah: The Lord Shall Provide; Jehovah-Rapha: The Lord Who Heals).

4. GOD IS STILL GOD

1. *"You'll never know what happened on that floor of St Jude's until you get to heaven,"* the oncologist said. *"The whole atmosphere changed; people were changed. They could all hear you singing, praising, and praying. It was like I saw a picture of what faith is."* What challenge does Jessica's example of faith present to you?

2. Jessica blamed herself when Keagan died. *"I should have tried to raise him from the dead. I hadn't even said, 'Live in Jesus' name' the way I'd planned. My son died on my watch."* As well as self-blame, what other natural and universal responses to grief are you aware of? Read 1 Thessalonians 4:13. Is Paul saying it's wrong to grieve? What always accompanies a Christian's grief?

3. *"I would not allow my faith to be shipwrecked. And I would never quit believing that Jesus is the healer."* In 1 Peter 1:13, what steps

will help prevent our faith from being shipwrecked? How can you be more intentional about implementing each step in your life?

4. A still, yet powerful voice said to Pete, *"This changes nothing."* He wrestled with it but knew it was true. What is your interpretation of this word from God? How did it help Pete and Jessica face the future? Recall a time when a word from God shifted your perspective.

5. Read the following scriptures, noting some of what Jesus did while here on earth.

   a. Matthew 9:2-8   b. Mark 1:21-28, 30-31

   c. Luke 7:22, 48   d. John 6:5-14

   e. John 9:1-7   f. Acts 10:38

6. Read Hebrews 13:8 and James 1:17. If you could ask Jesus to do one thing for you today, what would it be? Now take a moment to tell Him your request.

EXTRA STUDY: Make the most comprehensive list you can of the specific miracles of Jesus as recorded in the gospels. What does this teach us about the nature of God? Memorize Psalm 62:11-12 in your favorite version of the Bible.

5. WIDENING THE LENS

1. Read Matthew 8:5-13. What did Jesus say about the centurion's faith? Does having 'great faith' mean that we have no doubts? How does doubt differ from unbelief?

2. Jessica had doubts: *"Had my faith ultimately failed? Why did God not keep His end of the bargain? If Jesus is the Healer, why wasn't Keagan healed?"* Read Hebrews 11:1 and Hebrews 11:39. Do you feel comfortable talking to the Father about your doubts? Why

or why not? What do you do to build up your faith when your prayers aren't answered as you expected?

3. *"We run into trouble when our only answer to these questions is, 'God is in control—He is sovereign.'"* How could this explanation for suffering alone (i.e., discounting our fallen world and man's inhumanity to man) raise more questions than it answers?

4. *"The sovereignty of God does not refer to what God does or doesn't do, but who God fundamentally is. It's referring to the character of God."* What do you think about this statement? Find aspects of God's character in these verses:

    a. Numbers 23:19   b. Deuteronomy 32:4
    c. 1 Samuel 2:2   d. Psalm 25:8
    e. Psalm 34:8   f. Psalm 86:15
    g. Hebrews 10:23   h. James 1:17
    i. 1 John 1:5; 4:8   j   Revelation 19:11

5. *"In the kingdom of God, our own lives and situations matter, but there is always a bigger picture."* What can you do to partner with God when looking at the bigger picture of your situation?

6. Read Acts 1:4-8. In verse 6, the disciples asked a question. They were looking at their situation through their eyes, not the bigger picture. What was Jesus' answer to them, and how did it widen the lens?

EXTRA STUDY: Choose one member of the Trinity and do a more in-depth study on His nature. The more deeply you grow in your knowledge of the Father, Son, and Holy Spirit, the more you will fall in love with Him.

6. WHEN FAITH IS TESTED

1. Have you ever been told that God is testing your faith? What do the following scriptures say about this?
    a. James 1:13-14
    b. 2 Peter 2:9. Does it make sense for God to send a trial to you, and then have to rescue you from the trial that He sent?
    c. 1 Thessalonians 3:5. Who is Peter referring to as the tempter?

2. Read Luke 22:31-32. As well as life's circumstances testing us, this tells us that Satan desires to sift us like wheat. When something is sifted, it is shaken, often violently, to see what falls out. What was Satan's goal in 'sifting' Peter?

3. Notice that the above verse didn't say, "Satan desires to sift you like wheat, so here's how to avoid that." Is there a situation you wish you could avoid? What might Jesus be saying to you as you walk through this season?

4. In the original language, the word Jesus used for 'you' is plural, meaning 'all of you'. Satan desires to sift *all of you* like wheat, but I have prayed for *all of you* that your faith would not fail. Read John 17:20 and Romans 8:34. What confidence or comfort does it give you to know that Jesus is praying for you?

5. Confess to Jesus where you stand in your faith right now. You might say something like this: "Jesus, this trial feels really shaky and uncomfortable and hard, but I'm sticking with you. My faith and hope are in you."

6. *"Jesus prays that our faith will not fail because there are souls who need the hope and healing we can bring."* Which Christian testimonies of faith have most impacted you and why? (If you need inspiration,

think of people such as Adoniram Judson, Corrie Ten Boom, Joni Eareckson-Tada, and many hymn writers.)

EXTRA STUDY: Read or listen to some testimonies of men and women who carried a fierce faith in God's promises and dependence on Him amid dark trials—people who experienced deep doubts, but whose conviction did not fail.

7. ENCOUNTERING GOD

1. As is often the case with layers of grief, Jessica was back at the crossroads—either believe God's words or believe her feelings screaming that God had abandoned her. What are your feelings screaming at you?

2. Jessica told God, *"I feel like the devil came and spiritually raped me, and you stood by and did nothing! Where were you? Why didn't you come through?"* God knows that right on the tail of your accusation is a broken heart. What do you need to say to Him? Say it. Tell Him how you feel. Once you have, wait in silence before Him and listen for Him to speak to your heart.

3. The Greek word often used for the Holy Spirit is *paraklētos*—the one who comes alongside. Jessica writes: *"It's like you've fallen into a pit, and the Spirit has purposefully fallen in with you. He comes alongside and says, 'Let's get out of this pit together.'"* How could you deepen your intimacy with the Holy Spirit?

4. Read not just Jesus' words, but Jesus' heart in Matthew 7:7-11. Why is He stressing that we be so persistent in our relationship with the Father?

5. In Matthew 7:7-11, the original Greek implies to ask and *keep on* asking, seek and *keep on* seeking, knock and *keep on* knocking.

(The Amplified version word-for-word.) When your feelings are pushing you away from God, how hard is it for you to do the 'keep on' part? For encouragement, read Psalm 40. Notice the words 'waited patiently' in the first verse. How is God asking you to trust His timing?

6. Read the parable about a persistent widow in Luke 18:1-8. At the end of this parable, Jesus says, "When the Son of Man comes, will he find this kind of persistent faith on the earth?" (AMP). Will you have persistent faith? What do you envisage the evidence of persistent faith will look like in your life?

EXTRA STUDY: Knowing the promises in scripture is one thing. Deep down conviction that God will keep them is another. During the week, work through these questions with God: Do I believe you keep your promises? What promises are easy for me to believe you for? Which are hard for me to believe you for? What do I believe about your integrity? Ask the Spirit to show you what is at the root of any unbelief.

8. GRIEF UPON GRIEF

1. Jessica kept on seeking and asking God: *"What did I do wrong? Did I not have enough faith? Did I not pray enough? Was there some sin in my life that kept my prayers from being answered? Should I have done something different?"* Why didn't God answer her questions? Are there questions you've asked about your situation that could be in the same category as Jessica's?

2. *I realized it wasn't God who abandoned me; it was my family.* Jessica longed for the closeness with her mom that her mom could no longer provide. Why do we keep yearning for parental support,

even in cases where our childhood was marked by emotional neglect or conditional love?

3. *"Well, I don't know,"* Mom said to me. *"God rained down judgment on people in the Bible."*

   "You seriously think God took my son to teach me a lesson? . . . Just so you know, you're wrong." From Jessica's story, what have you learned about what to say and not to say to grieving people?

4. *"I was not going to give my mom permission to speak into my life on that topic anymore."*

   Read:

       a. Isaiah 50:4   b. Proverbs 12:18

       c. Proverbs 15:4; 23   d. Proverbs 25:11

       e. Ephesians 4:29

   Who are the people you allow to speak into your life? If you need to put boundaries in place between yourself and someone who is pulling you down with their words, how will you do that?

5. *"The people from our church had become our family. God hadn't left us alone. We'd been surrounded by people who had loved us the way I'd needed my family to love us."* Who has God placed in your life for this season?

6. What is the sure promise from God to you in James 1:5? Have you asked God for His wisdom in what to say and how to handle your situation?

EXTRA STUDY: Think of the people who are in your corner—the spiritual parents/grandparents/siblings who build you up in faith. During the next week, encourage them by letting them know how much they mean to you.

9. OPENING THE FLOODGATES

1. *"Reading the Bible felt like walking through a desert. Prayer felt dry, barren, and fruitless."* Read Proverbs 13:12. Have you ever walked through a dry, desolate time when your hope was crushed? How did God meet you during that period?

2. Read the account of the disciples on the road to Emmaus in Luke 24:13-53. How ironic that they asked the only one who knew everything this question: "Are you the only stranger visiting Jerusalem who is unaware of the things which have happened here?" What were the disciples hoping for (v. 21)? How did Jesus describe their mindset (v. 25)?

3. Notice that when Jesus opened their eyes to the truth, the disciples turned their hearts toward others. How could you turn your heart toward others while in your own time of trial?

4. Have you taken time to ask the Holy Spirit to fall into the pit with you? Have you invited Him into your grief?

5. Read James 4:7-8. The definition of action is 'something that is done, not merely thought or spoken about'. In verse 7, what are the two opposite 'actions' we must do? From verse 8, what will be the result of our actions? As you pray and seek God, you are drawing near to him. Expect Him to draw near to you!

6. *"I want my son back! You don't understand, Jesus. You never got married and had kids. As a parent, kids are connected to our heart, and you wouldn't understand that."* What revelation did Jesus give Jessica in answer to her broken heart? Why do you think it made her love Jesus more than ever?

EXTRA STUDY: Most often, we study the works of Jesus while He was in human form on earth. This week, explore the present work of Jesus. Explore

His ministry now, at this moment, in both heaven and on earth (e.g., What is He doing now as our High Priest, Head of the Church, Bridegroom?)

10. RUN THE RACE

1. *"There was a lot about Pete's grief I didn't pick up on at the time."* How can a lack of outward signs of grief in one partner cause tension in a marriage? What could cause men to grieve differently from women?

2. Why did Pete's vision put the wind back in their sails and shift their perspective? What has been your experience of receiving visions from God?

3. What do you think about the pastor's advice? *"You need to grieve. But grief can hang on and on. It can keep you stuck, and depression stems from that. We're not trying to hurry you along. But we are cautioning you as we walk the road of grief that this can happen. You don't want to get stuck here."* What principles have you learned from Jessica's experience that would help you get unstuck?

4. Explore the following scriptures to learn what it means to run well:
   a. 1 Corinthians 9:24-27. We all run, and we should run to obtain the prize. What does Paul list as requirements for winning, and how could you apply those to your situation?
   b. 2 Timothy 4:7. How do running your race well and keeping the faith go together?
   c. Galatians 5:7. Who or what is preventing you from running well?
   d. Philippians 3:13-14. What are some healthy things you can do to press toward the goal?
   e. Hebrews 12:1-2. What weight could you strip off to help you run? What does endurance and persistence mean to you?

5. According to the following verses, how did Jesus run the race set by His Father?

    a. Luke 9:51   b. Hebrews 12:2

    c. Philippians 2:5-8

What comfort does it bring you, knowing that Jesus has also run the race before you?

6. *Even as I write this book, my son is cheering me on. "Mom! This is helping someone today! Keep writing! Write through the tears and the hard things. Someone will read this and receive healing and have the courage to run their race!"* What hope and encouragement has Jessica's story brought you if deep grief has been part of your journey? Have you thought about how your story might help others find meaning after loss?

EXTRA STUDY: Jessica writes, "Running well is a theme embedded in our family's DNA . . . At the end of the year, each graduate picked a 'life verse'. Reece picked Hebrews 12:1." Think about potential advantages of selecting a family life verse: fostering spiritual growth, encouraging family conversations, shaping daily choices, building a mindset of helping others. Is choosing a life verse something you would consider for your family? If so, how would you choose?

11. FIGHTING THE FEAR

1. Daily, paralyzing fear overtook Jessica: *What if Pete dies? What if Reece dies? What if I die? What if my best friend dies? I found myself playing out scenarios, trying to make a plan for how I would deal with each one."* What scriptures helped Jessica recognize the difference between grief and her thought life running amok?

2. Read Mark 14:33-35 and Luke 22:44. Describe some of the emotions Jesus was feeling. Do you think He was experiencing fear? If so, explain.

3. How open was Jesus with His Father about His feelings? What does this teach us?

4. What fears are you currently dealing with? Imagine Jesus coming to your house and sitting with you. What words of love would He speak to you?

5. What pictures or thoughts have dominated your mind? Have they been good or bad? Read Philippians 4:8. What pictures and thoughts would Jesus have you think on?

6. Jessica's fear went beyond the natural grieving process. It was more than her thoughts running wild. She was in a battle against a spirit of fear. Note all the action words in Ephesians 6:10-18 (e.g., 'be strong', 'put on'). Also note words and phrases that indicate we are in battle (e.g., 'armour', 'stand against'). Does anything in this scripture suggest that we can live a passive Christian life? Where do you need to 'suit up' and take up your authority in Christ?

EXTRA STUDY: Write a descriptive scene of yourself free from your struggles. What does your face look like? How do you feel? Describe what would be going on around you. Are there family and friends around you? Laughter? Music? Be as descriptive as you can. What things in that scene are praiseworthy? Of good report? Lovely? Pure and wholesome, and bring peace? Remember to think on THOSE things.

12. STRENGTH TO ENDURE

1. Why is it difficult for leaders to be honest and vulnerable about their challenges?

2. *"We must not confuse what we are going through with who we are."* Even knowing David would commit adultery and murder, what did God say his identity was? (1 Samuel 13:14; Acts 13:22). Knowing that Peter would deny Him, what did Jesus say Peter's identity was? (Matthew 16:18). Scripture reveals our identity in Christ. Who do you allow to define your identity?

3. What is your testimony? I was _____ but now I'm _____. What testimony are you believing God for?

4. Identify your own area of greatest weakness. Perhaps it's people pleasing, lack of affection, stinginess, or lack of compassion. What would it look like if God turned that area into a strength?

5. Read 2 Corinthians 12:7-10. Pray, asking God to show Himself strong in your weaknesses.

6. *I remember singing, "You have turned my mourning into dancing, and my sorrow into joy." I didn't feel that way. I sang at my weakest point, and God became strong inside of me.* From Hebrews 13:15, what does a 'sacrifice of praise' look like? What does the word 'sacrifice' teach us about praising God when we don't feel like it?

EXTRA STUDY: From the following scriptures, discover examples of the profound power of praise and worship: 2 Chronicles 20:1-24; Joshua 6:1-16; Acts 16:25-26. Have you ever thought of worship as a spiritual weapon? What can you do in your own home to increase your worship?

13. ENCOURAGING YOURSELF IN THE LORD

1. *"There's a joy that comes with encouraging yourself in the Lord that's like nothing anyone else or any other environment can bring."* 1 Samuel 30:1-6 gives the account of where King David's men threatened to

stone him, yet he 'encouraged himself in the Lord' (v. 6). When your peace is under threat, what do you do to encourage yourself in the Lord?

2. David's life pattern was to turn to God through prayer and worship in challenging times. How does this reflect his identity as 'a man after God's own heart'? Who (or what screen) do you turn to first to find encouragement when you've lost peace? How can you more deeply aspire to be a man or woman after God's own heart?

3. *"Trees provide shade for others; shelter for others; food for others."* Isaiah 61:3 references God's people as "trees of righteousness, the planting of the Lord, that He may be glorified." From this verse, what does God do for us so that our lives can glorify Him?

4. Sometimes we don't feel like encouraging ourselves, but this is when we need to do so the most. Even if it feels dry or pointless, encourage yourself anyway. The Holy Spirit will come alongside you and help you. Ask Him to!

5. Write out scriptures or statements that encourage you in Christ. Read them out loud and confess them over yourself. Let yourself hear your voice proclaiming victory!

6. What does it look like for you to be on the other side of your situation? What will it feel like? What will you look like? Confess those things NOW while you are in the middle of your trial!

EXTRA STUDY: Read Jeremiah 17:7-8, where the prophet uses the image of a mature and thriving tree to paint a graphic picture of the characteristics of the person who trusts in the Lord. If your longing is to draw more sustenance from the stream of God's love and to bear more fruit to glorify Him, ask the Holy Spirit what is on His heart for your growth and ministry.

14. RELAXING INTO THE LOVE OF GOD

1. *"Resting in the love of God is the deepest expression of faith during trials. We may still need to bail water out of the boat, but we do so from a place of peace, trust, and relaxation into the love of God."* What are your thoughts about this comment? When have you experienced deep peace while a storm (literal or figurative!) raged around you?

2. The ultimate evidence that God makes a way for us is the sacrifice of Jesus. *"God has already looked around the corners of your life, and He's already made a way."* From Psalm 23, list all the ways Jesus is going ahead of you, making a way through the mountains and valleys in your life.

3. *"Knowing the character of God is helpful to us. Reading the Bible is important too. But there's an intangible element called the leading of the Holy Spirit which we cannot live without."* What are your reflections on this statement? In the following scriptures, note the work of the Holy Spirit.

   a. Acts 8:29
   b. Acts 10:19
   c. Acts 13:2-4
   d. Acts 16:6–7
   e. Acts 20:22–23

   Romans 5:5 says, "Now hope does not disappoint, because the love of God has been poured out in our hearts by the Holy Spirit who was given to us." How well do you know the person and work of the Holy Spirit who is gifted to you?

4. In what areas of your life do you want God to have mercy on you? Ask Him for His mercy right now. Where is God inviting you to turn your focus away from yourself and extend mercy to another?

5. Jessica used an illustration of driving a race car and the concept of "You go where you look." Where have you been looking? Do you need to adjust your focus?

6. God provided a ram so that Abraham didn't have to sacrifice his son, Isaac. Abraham named that place, "The Lord Provides." What struggle have you come through with God? What will you call that place? If you haven't come through your struggle yet, what will you call it when you do?

EXTRA STUDY: Find a quiet spot for an uninterrupted time with God. Does He have your trust? If not, where do you believe He has failed you? God knows your every struggle. You can be honest with Him. He doesn't walk away. What worry do you need to release to Him? Pour out your heart to Him. Write out and/or memorize Psalm 91:1-2.

15. THE OVERFLOW OF COMPASSION

1. David didn't say, "*If* I am afraid." He said, "*When* I am afraid, I will put my trust and faith in You." (Psalm 56:3). Trusting God in our fears enables us to run our race and help others in theirs. Has someone you know been sidelined in their race? Ask the Holy Spirit to show you how to encourage them (1 Thessalonians 5:11).

2. "*What makes compassion so powerful is that it is fundamentally practical.*" Write down the names of people who came to mind when you were reading this chapter. What practical things can you do to help lighten their load?

3. "*Did you change the world today?*" Read John 14:8-14. What does Jesus say that those who believe in Him will do?

4. *"We're all given different gifts and abilities so we can partner with God for the thing that moves His heart."* Look at the list at the end of chapter 15. What stirs your heart the most? What are you passionate about? Ask God what He wants you to do about this today.

5. What does 1 Peter 5:9 teach about our shared experiences? Who could benefit from your experience if you were to tell your story?

6. "I have stored up your word in my heart, that I might not sin against you" (Psalm 119:11 ESV). In general, what does it mean to 'store' things up? Read Hebrews 4:12. How does this verse describe God's Word? Is it just information? Now that you've completed these studies, what will you put in place to 'keep on' storing up God's Word in your heart?

EXTRA STUDY: "For Jesus, action always flowed from compassion." Take some time and go through the gospels. Look at the miracles Jesus did and how He interacted with people. Ask Him to allow you to see others through His eyes. Ask Him to put His words in your mouth to speak to others.

Tributes to Keagan

Keagan was a beautiful child. He had eyes the color of faded blue jeans, he loved to pretend play and be Spiderman, Batman, Superman, Bible man, and Larry Boy (from Veggie Tales). He was on the artistic side of things and could draw a picture of Larry Boy at two years old that was very recognizable. Sometimes I had to get on to him because he would get up after we had put him to bed and put socks on his hands, snow boots on his feet, and this stocking cap with ear flaps. He was pretending to be a boxer, but he would fall asleep with that stuff on. I would wake him up in the morning and uncover him and see it all. His feet would be shriveled from sweating all night in those boots. He didn't like to go outside very much because he didn't like bugs, but he loved trips to Silver Dollar City with our family. He loved to laugh! At his fourth birthday party, we got him a whoopee cushion and it was the hit of the party. I never saw him laugh so hard in my life! He was an easy child, always so loving and kind. He had a friend at church who was two years younger than him, and this child would push him and hit him. We told him that he needed to push him back, but he just wasn't that kind of kid. He didn't have the heart to do it. I was deeply touched when a friend, Jeanene Sutton, wrote a poem about Keagan, which we displayed at his funeral. She captured his personality and who he was perfectly:

Little Boy Dreams

Superheroes reigned supreme
in Keagan's little boy dreams
A sword and hat were all it took
to be Peter Pan or Captain Hook
A purple cape close at hand
turned Keagan into Bible Man
"Mom and Dad, even though I try
I don't understand why I can't fly."
Just why Keagan had to go
The secret things we can not know
But in heaven, wherever little boys play
I can almost hear him say,
"Mom and Dad, look at me
I'm everything I dreamed I'd be."

Looking at pictures of Keagan and me, it's strange how familiar yet distant they feel. There we are together in the same frame, but the memories don't come as easily as I wish they would. It's like seeing a version of myself that I should remember, but don't. I've mourned him, even if my mourning doesn't look the same as my mom or dad. Maybe it's been more of a quiet ache, a longing for something I was too young to hold onto. It's grieving the moments I don't remember, but I know I must have had. It's feeling the weight of his absence in stories, in the way my parents say his name, in the spaces he should still fill. I may not have all the memories, but I do have the love, and I think in some way, that is its own kind of remembering. The times that really hurt the most are hearing the hurt of my parents, but I also see the happiness they have telling stories and sharing how God moved in my brother's situation, and knowing his story will help others and will bring healing to those who are hurting.

—Reece

I have grown up knowing I have a brother, but won't know him here on this earth. It's heartbreaking to me because this is someone that I should know and have a deep relationship with, but I have no memories of him. I know him through my parents' stories, and pictures. He's almost like a stranger to me when he should be known to me as a brother and close friend. I mourn what should have been. I mourn not knowing his personality, his sense of humor, his thoughts and dreams. I mourn the moments we would have had together as a family. I know we'll be together for eternity, but until then, I look forward to seeing how many lives are changed and helped because of his story.

—Charis

Acknowledgments

To my son, Reece. You were the smiling baby boy who made me want to live back then and the strong young man who encouraged me to write this book today.

For my daughter, Charis. Thanks for encouraging me to write this story so that it lives beyond me.

For my husband, Pete. We have weathered the storms of life together and there is no one who understands me like you do.

To Pastor Guy Johnston. Your gift to teach the Word built a strong foundation in our lives and that foundation has held fast through the storms of life.

To my editor and publisher, Anya McKee. Thanks for keeping me focused and teaching me how to write this book.

About the Author

To follow Jessica or to invite her to speak at your event, please visit:

www.jessicalongspeaks.com

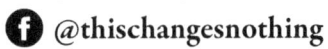 **@thischangesnothing**

www.ingramcontent.com/pod-product-compliance
Lightning Source LLC
Chambersburg PA
CBHW061759120626
46550CB00005B/2053